ANTIQUES AT HOME

Also by Barbara Milo Ohrbach

The Scented Room

A Token of Friendship

Memories of Childhood

Barbara Milo Ohrbach

Antiques At Home

CHERCHEZ'S BOOK OF COLLECTING AND DECORATING WITH ANTIQUES

Photographs by John Hall   Text with Martina D'Alton

DOUBLEDAY

SYDNEY   LONDON   AUCKLAND   NEW YORK   TORONTO

The engravings on the endpapers for this book
are by F. Bartolozzi R.A. and P. W. Tomkins,
from *The Seasons* by James Thomlon, London, 1797.
The ornamental engravings at the end of each chapter
are from *Collection de Meubles et Objets de Goût*
by Pierre de la Mésangère, Paris, 1825.

Design by Rochelle Udell

Grateful acknowledgment is made to Houghton Mifflin Company for permission
to reprint an excerpt from HOME BEFORE DARK by Susan Cheever.
Copyright © 1984 by Susan Cheever. Reprinted by permission of the publisher
and the author. Lines from "Nineteen Hundred and Nineteen" are reproduced
with permission of Macmillan Publishing Co., from *The Poems of W. B. Yeats:
A New Edition,* edited by Richard J. Finneran.
© 1928 by Macmillan Publishing Co., renewed 1956 by Georgie Yeats.

Published in Australasia in 1989 by Doubleday, a division of Transworld Publishers (Aust.) Pty Limited,
15–23 Helles Avenue, Moorebank NSW 2170
Published in Great Britain in 1989 by Doubleday, a division of Transworld Publishers Limited,
61–3 Uxbridge Road, London W5 5SA
Published by arrangement with Clarkson N. Potter, Inc., 201 East 50th Street, New York, New York 10022.

National Library of Australia
Cataloguing-in-Publication data
Ohrbach, Barbara Milo.
  Antiques at home: Cherchez's book of
collecting and decorating with antiques.
Bibliography.
Includes index.
ISBN 0 86824 393 0.
1. Antiques. 2. Antiques in interior decoration.
I. Hall, John. II. D'Alton, Martina. III. Cherchez
(Firm). IV. Title.
745.1

British Library Cataloguing
in Publication data
Ohrbach, Barbara Milo
  Antiques at home: a book of
collecting and decorating with
antiques.
1. Antiques. Collecting
I. Title
745.1'075
ISBN 0-385-26996-X

Many ingenious lovely things are gone
That seemed sheer miracle to the multitude . . .
WILLIAM BUTLER YEATS

To anyone who has rescued a neglected
object and cherished it,
tried to save a venerable building,
or spent an afternoon sharing an older person's memories,
to all who find warmth and lasting beauty in the old,
this book is dedicated.

Thank you to my father, who took us to museums and historic places from the moment we could walk. He taught us to respect and appreciate old things and always encouraged our curiosity.

Thank you to everyone who worked on *Antiques at Home*. A book takes the involvement of so many people. I am grateful to each one listed here for their enthusiasm and support. Special thanks to—

Carol Southern, Carolyn Hart Bryant, Gretchen Salisbury, Gael Towey, Barbara Peck, Ann Cahn, Kay Riley, and all the talented people at Clarkson N. Potter. I wish I could mention everyone by name.

Martina D'Alton, John Hall, and Rochelle Udell—it was a special pleasure to work with each of these exceptional individuals.

Deborah Geltman and Gayle Benderoff, who were there when I needed them.

Lisa Fresne, whose cheerful nature helped me maintain my momentum.

Jane Rappeport and Clare Thomas, who smoothed the way both here and abroad.

All the kind people who generously shared their time, knowledge, and treasures with me—Jules Arthur and Judith Hoffman Corwin; Susan Benjamin; Ann Marie Benson; Doris Leslie Blau; Joanna Booth; Ivan and the late Alice Bryden; Nina Campbell; Russell Carrell; the staff at Colefax and Fowler; Antigone Clarke; Geoffrey and Val Cridland; Madeleine Donahue; Paul Duncan; M. E. Evans; Richard L. Feigen; the Forbes Magazine Galleries; Martin and Prue Lane Fox; Suzie Frankfort; Richard and Susan Gaskell; Henry Greenfield; Betty Gunter; Robert and Susan Gunter; Mark and Duane Hampton; Patricia Harvey; Christopher Hodsoll; Ed and Anita Holden; Jonathan Horne; the Honorable Mr. and Mrs. Simon Howard and the staff of Castle Howard, York; David Howard; Paul Jones; Don Kelley and Warren Fitzsimmons, The Captain Jefferds Inn; Jilly Kelly; Margaret Kelly; the Kennebunkport Inn; Heather Schorr King; Vi Koerner; Evelyn Kraus; Alice Kwartler; Ann LeConey; Stephen Long; Jesse McNab; Millie Manheim; William McCoombe; the late J. Garvin Mecking; Elinor Merrell; Charlotte Moss; Edward and Norma Munves; Barbara R. Munves; Maria Neforos; Gilly Newberry; Edwin Palko; Christine Palmer; John Partridge; the textile department at Phillips Fine Auctioneers; Trevor and Pam Potts; Roger Prigent; Antoinette Putnam; Dennis Rolland; Antonia Salvato; Charles and Cynthia Salzhauer; the Schaefer family; Dennis Severs; Julian and Carolyn Sheffield; the Trustees of Sir John Soane's Museum; Alastair Stair; Lynne Stair; Barbara Sutherland; Gerry Tandy; John and Faith Tompkins; Aasha Tyrrell; Paul R. Vandekar; Helene Von Rosenstiel; William Washburn; Cindy Watson; Barry M. Witmond; Angus Wilkie; Peter and Toni Wing; Melissa Wyndham.

Mel, whose long-shared love of old things has made this book possible.

Lastly, thanks to all of you who have read my books and written the most wonderful letters. They inspire me.

CONTENTS

Introduction

By a subtle and inevitable process, the man who cares for his house can easily become a collector.

An Illustrated History of
Interior Decoration,
Mario Praz

On the table before me is a bowl of old ceramic carpet balls, their intriguing patterns and colors glowing in the sunlight. They've occupied the same spot in our living room for almost fifteen years. And like many of the objects in our home, this nineteenth-century game reminds me of the wonderful trips we've taken and the times we've had collecting antiques.

My husband and I bought the carpet balls during a long weekend we spent exploring Scotland. We found them in a tiny antiques shop near Aberdeen, nestled in their own hand-carved wooden bowl lined with a needlework doily. The little chips and nicks on their smooth surfaces seemed to reflect many hours of use in a Victorian parlor a century earlier. We couldn't resist—not allowing ourselves to think about the fact that the balls were fragile, very heavy, and would have to be hand-carried through many more countries and two weeks of work before heading home. They sit here now with Christmas cards and invitations tucked among them. And I know when our nieces and nephews come to visit, they always want to play with them, much as the original owners must have done so many years ago.

Beautiful antiques that were used and loved in everyday life in the past have become very special, even important, to many of us today. These objects were designed

Our ceramic carpet balls, called carpet bowls in Great Britain, nestled in their own wooden bowl, on a 19th-century wool tartan throw from Scotland.

and made to last at a time when quality, materials, and workmanship were all.

As it was for the Victorians, whose homes were a refuge from the industrialization growing around them, for many of us today, home means a place where we can be comfortable away from the frenzied demands of modern life. We want it to be a place filled with warmth and permanence, reflecting the hearts of the people who live there. And with family members living farther and farther away from each other, the familiar objects that connect us —the silver porringer that has been in the family for generations or the cut-glass vase that belonged to Mother—become even more significant. These objects link us with the past and give us a sense of continuity that has become most important in a sometimes very impersonal world.

That is what this book is all about— collecting, living with, and decorating with small antiques—the china teapot on the sideboard that you inherited from your great-aunt, the inlaid wood lap desk with all its original fittings that you bought when you first discovered you loved old objects, or the basket you picked up last summer at your favorite antiques show. This is not meant to be an encyclopedia of antiques but rather one person's view—a personal view, practical, too, I hope—of the small treasures from the past that I love best. These objects give a room its personality and style—and a house its soul.

There is a human appeal to an object that was made by hand. I wonder about the person or people who made it. What were they thinking? What problems did

Left: *This American basket, hand-woven over a hundred years ago, retains its wonderful crisp texture.*
Right: *A harmonious grouping of objects— Meissen figurines, an Italian bronze, enamel boxes—collected by different generations, look very much at home atop a Georgian satinwood table.*

they have? What was their life like? The fact that something has survived intact all these years, that we are able to appreciate and be refreshed by it and pass it on, is reassuring. I read recently about how Sir Kenneth Clark, the esteemed British art historian, started collecting old things. He said that at first he bought them from "a sentimental feeling that I must rescue them from neglect." It's such a lovely thought. I think we all should do what we can to preserve the wonderful old buildings and objects that are still left. We should treasure and respect the old—old people, too!

Another reason so many of us are turning to antiques to furnish their homes is the sheer beauty of them. "Things of quality have no fear of time" is printed on a little card I've had pinned above my desk for ages. I'm the first to agree that not everything old is of the highest aesthetic or material quality. So much *is*, though, that it is a joy just to keep searching. We get something special from fine objects every time we look at them—the creativity, meticulous craftsmanship, and spirit shine through. At last we have begun to realize that these things will never be made in the same way again. As a result, today there is a trend to collect antiques that is widespread and growing.

Technically, an antique is an object made over one hundred years ago. Because this was established in 1930 by the U.S. government to determine import laws for antiques, 1830 is the date used by many people as the definition of an antique, but to my mind either is acceptable.

When I first started collecting, I felt guilty if I bought something solely because it was decorative and I adored it. Shouldn't I be more intellectual than this? I thought. Shouldn't it be something more, have historical importance, be rare, or by some famous maker? Yes and no. Good design, craftsmanship, and condition are very important.

Of course, you should be as discern-

Above: *Summer means gardening and swimming but, best of all, finding antiques at outdoor country shows.*
Left: *I couldn't resist the perfume sign, perfect for Cherchez, any more than I could the old gate. Don't ask what I will do with it, but I know it will come in handy someday.*

ing and knowledgeable as you can be, whether or not you are spending large sums of money. In fact, one of the benefits of antiques collecting is that you become very curious about these objects. Where was it made? When? By whom? You start going to specialized little museums, some started by people then considered eccentrics or by farsighted individuals who collected the same things that you do now. Reference books on the subject become prized possessions themselves. But none of this is more important than the object itself, which, whether it is a kitchen utensil or a rare paperweight, is something that you should buy because you will enjoy living with it from day to day.

Every expert I spoke to when I was researching this book told me the same thing, something I eventually learned myself: Buy what you love—antiques are a passionate pastime. Edmond de Goncourt, an eminent French collector, once said, "If you ever take up collecting, each time you are tempted by a work of art, by a curio, be sure to ask yourself before deciding to buy: Can I live with it, keep it in front of my eyes, and love it until I die? Believe me, there is no better touchstone."

In an article in a favorite English magazine, I read about a woman's obsession with antiques. She wondered if there were not some form of therapy available to people like herself who cannot safely be allowed out of the house in case they come back bearing an embroidered fire screen. She confided, "I go off to do ordinary shopping, and find myself in antiques shops." I don't find anything wrong with her—it happens to me all the time!

I think, if you talk to anyone who loves antiques, they will be most enthusiastic about the quest for their treasures. Never before have there been so many events at which this passion can be indulged—auctions, antiques shows, tag sales, and flea markets have sprung up everywhere. There is always another wonderful antique lurking around the corner, inspiring a never-ending feeling that the best is yet to come. Like so many other collectors, I plan vacations and business trips to coincide with auctions and antiques shows. Getting up at 4:30 A.M. on a winter morning is no problem when I know I'm going to Bermondsey, an outdoor market in London in which I have found the most fabulous things. It seems to me that dealers and collectors are some of the most vital and ageless people I know. Perhaps it's their boundless curiosity and endless searching that makes them so.

My passion for collecting began with a group of paper dolls when I was a little girl. Happy summer afternoons were spent with my friends poring over our collections and trading them as the boys did baseball cards. Of course, I thought mine were the best—after all, I had almost all the famous Hollywood actresses *plus* the Toni twins with a wardrobe of wigs in every fifties hairstyle imaginable.

I stored the cutouts in a big red Macy's box, keeping the fragile paper outfits between sheets of wax paper. I used so much that I was finally given my own roll of Cut-Rite strictly for this purpose. My parents moved when I was in college and the paper dolls disappeared. But writing this now, I can still picture Piper Laurie and June Allyson in the most gorgeous tulle evening gowns ever, with matching shoes, bag, and wrap.

Each year my family took a trip at Easter time. My father planned it months ahead, always to someplace historic—Gettysburg, Mt. Vernon, Old Sturbridge Village, Williamsburg. Aside from the Shirley Temple cocktails we were allowed to order at dinner, the highlights of these trips were the little hand-blown glass pitchers that my sister and I would always pick out in the souvenir shops—another collection in the making to be displayed on my dressing table. I was also developing an abiding love of museums and the past to be tucked away and emerge years later. Then I went off to college and stopped collecting. In fact, from then until I moved back to New York, I was proud of the fact that I could fit all that I owned into a single trunk—well, almost.

Once I started working in the fashion industry, I found myself traveling to Europe several times a year. Gradually, I felt that familiar pull, and in my off hours I haunted the flea markets of Paris, London, and Rome. You could find really wonderful things then. My first collection was antique boxes of all kinds. And, perhaps because of my involvement in fashion, I also

 Two of my collections, started long ago and still favorites.
Above right: *Victorian linens tied with satin ribbons with weighted sachet flowers at each end.*
Right: *English Staffordshire cups, plates, and serving pieces in my china cupboard.*

had an interest in old textiles. Soon our closets were overflowing with Kashmir shawls, bits of old lace, early eighteenth-century printed cottons, Kossu robes, and pieces of Regency needlework. On weekends and summers in the country, I would scour flea markets and antiques fairs.

When my husband, Mel, and I decided to open Cherchez, our shop, it was almost as though we had been planning to do just that all along. We had more than enough to stock the shelves. I like to think that visiting Cherchez is like opening an old trunk in an attic—there is a serendipity to it, a surprise on every shelf.

Flowers in art first appeared in sixth-century manuscripts on medicinal plants and since then have been a favored theme in all the decorative arts. Flowers are a kind of theme in both my collecting and in the shop. I am drawn to flowers painted on old china, embroidered on silk sam-

 Little still lifes around the house are composed of my small collections.
Clockwise from above left: *A cluster of 19th-century jugs with floral and gardening motifs, the largest holding a bunch of dried hydrangeas.*
Delicate little watercolors and framed trade-cards surround a mirror.
A robust Clematis jackmanii, *in bloom on the porch on a lazy summer's day.*
Old-fashioned roses from our garden flanked by pink and copper luster saucers on the mantelpiece.
Overleaf: *It doesn't matter whether you have a dear collection of little mugs or something quite a bit grander . . .*
Above: *The china cabinet at Castle Howard in York, England, was designed with the house in the early 18th century by architect John Vanbrugh. It holds a very large collection of several china services, including Meissen Red Dragon and Crown Derby botanicals, all collected by the family over the years.*
Below: *A small collection of children's mugs decorated with children playing and words of wisdom.*

Rewards of merit were often given to schoolchildren for work well done. They were also given as awards at art shows, music recitals, and other competitions. Engraved in silver with graceful lettering and designs, they were highly prized and are still treasured today. This award, with its lovely flowery motif, is a rare find, and was probably given at a flower show or agricultural fair.

plers, engraved in fine old books, carved as architectural details on buildings.

Those of you who are familiar with my first book, *The Scented Room*, know I love flowers—especially the real ones. Although here too I prefer the antique. In the book I talked at length about our old-fashioned shrub roses and herbs. Now my husband and I are busy filling in the orchards on our property with old varieties of apple trees. Many of these, once popular, had fallen from favor only to be rediscovered recently by people who want to preserve the old species for future generations. A revival of interest in the past is happening everywhere around us.

This book has given me an opportunity to see some very beautiful homes and objects. In doing so, I have been able to talk to many experts—both collectors and dealers—in the world of antiques. Their enthusiasm has been infectious, and, I hope, will come through in every chapter. They enjoy what they do and have all been very generous in sharing their expertise with me. The limitations of time meant that I could not interview or photograph everybody or everything I wished to—I could have gone on forever!

I have arranged the chapters according to materials—"Ceramics," including porcelain, pottery, and enamels; "Wood," "Silver," "Textiles," where I talk about everything from quilts to old lace; "Glass," and "Paper," including prints and silhouettes. Each is a vast category, covered in great detail in books specifically on the subject. I have tried to make *Antiques at Home* practical, including inventive ideas for decorating and entertaining using antiques, plus discussions about the particular items, where to find the best quality, and what to look for.

And, while it is a privilege to own all these special things, it is also a responsibility. Since you are the custodian of them only as long as you own them, they should be passed on in as good a condition as possible. In each chapter there is a special section on caring for and maintaining your antiques. These methods, used by professionals in the museum and restoration worlds, have been adapted so that you can use them in your home.

Chapter Seven, "A Personal View," will give you a glimpse of how others have made their passion for antiques a part of their environments and includes a list of distinctive and unusual museums.

Because I have loved art and antiques almost all my life, Chapter Eight, "The Collector's World," is filled with particular inside information. There you will find lists of my favorite antiques shops and galleries, antiques shows and fairs, international antiques markets, auction houses, and flea markets. It also includes decorative arts and preservation societies, decorating and antiques magazines, and reference books, as well as conservators and restorers. I loved putting this chapter together and I hope you will enjoy using it as a guide in your antiques adventures.

Sometimes people are inhibited by feeling they don't have the knowledge, the time, or the money to have beautiful antiques in their lives. And that's wrong. You can have a small grouping of objects, two or three nice old plates on a shelf, perhaps, and that's a little collection. It enriches the room—and you, every time you look at it.

Even if you're not that famous Early American furniture collector you just read about who paid millions at auction for one chair or that man who collects old master paintings and has his own museum in California, you should not be put off enjoying or collecting antiques. They lend grace to our homes and lift our spirits. The joy of living with beautiful objects is accessible to all of us.

Barbara Milo Ohrbach
New York City

CHAPTER I
CERAMICS

It is the loveliness of little things that imparts life to a room, and ceramics are one of the very best examples of this. Just bringing a beautiful old, painted porcelain vase into a room and doing nothing more than setting it on a table can have the same effect as arranging a bouquet of fresh flowers in the space. The room is transformed. You are refreshed by the sight of a pleasing motif on the china, perhaps, or just by its shape and color, or by the glow of its glaze. There's magic in it.

If you collect ceramics, you have the opportunity to create this magic again and again, changing and shaping a room as your collection grows or simply as your mood changes. You also become part of a long, rich tradition. Ceramics have been prized since ancient times, when the Romans coveted beautiful Greek vases and displayed them in their homes.

Ancient pottery may be outside the budget of most of us. However, there is still a wide range of wonderful ceramic wares that are available and should be treasured, whether they are tremendously valuable or humbly ordinary. After all, though many were made purely for decoration, most were made for everyday use.

Collectors eventually become very knowledgeable about the things they collect. With ceramics this starts with the most basic questions: what are they made of, what are the different types, where were they made and when?

As in many fields, terminology can be confusing. The nature of the clays and glazes that makes a piece of ceramic so beautiful can be highly technical. If you become interested in unraveling the mysteries of this aspect of ceramics, there are many excellent books to turn to.

Without getting too technical, there are a few basics that everyone who appreciates ceramics should know. The first is the difference between porcelain and pottery. Most true porcelain is translucent. You can hold a piece of it up to a bright light and it will positively glow. Pottery, on the other hand, is opaque—it does not allow light to pass through it.

Porcelain, or china, is made of kaolin (white china clay virtually free of impurities) and other substances. It is nonporous, of a whitish color, and has great strength and hardness. There are two types of porcelain, hard paste and soft paste. Soft-paste porcelain is the result of early European potters' experiments with all sorts of materials in their search for the true porcelain made by the Chinese. By adding ground glass to the clay body, European potters obtained a certain translucency, but the finished pieces were neither as dense nor as hard as true porcelain. For this reason, they came to be called soft paste. Very beautiful but extremely fragile, soft-paste porcelain of the eighteenth century is today even rarer than true porcelain of the same era and is often more highly prized by collectors. Most eighteenth-century English porcelain and early Sèvres pieces are soft paste.

Hard-paste porcelain is simply another way of saying true porcelain. It was first made in China more than a thousand

Previous page: *A breakfast set of Minton china with transfer-printed designs of shells and seaweed that vary from piece to piece.*
Above left: *A New Milford lettuce-leaf pottery pitcher, made about 1870 in Connecticut. The shapes and colors of this distinctive American pottery make it very desirable to collect and use.*
Right: *A collection of New Milford pottery set within a richly carved 19th-century Portuguese rosewood cabinet. The dishes of assorted sizes are especially beautiful when used to serve desserts, such as fresh fruit or pale-colored sorbets.*

years ago and imported into Europe in the fifteenth century. Right from the beginning, the Europeans recognized and appreciated the high quality of this Chinese porcelain. True porcelain has always been considered the queen of ceramics, sought after and treasured. The European formula for its manufacture was finally arrived at in the early eighteenth century by Johann Friedrich Böttger, working at Meissen. All Chinese and most European porcelains from the mid-eighteenth century onward are hard paste.

Some of the most famous European porcelain factories that we know today were founded at that time: Meissen in Germany; St. Cloud, Chantilly, Mennecy, and Sèvres in France; Chelsea, Bow, Derby, Lowestoft, Worcester, Plymouth, and Bristol in England; and Nove, Doccia, and Capodimonte in Italy. These are just some of the names you should know if you are collecting porcelain.

Pottery is a term used to describe items of baked clay that without their glaze would be porous. They may be sunbaked or fired in kilns at high temperatures. Their color after firing depends on the constituents of the clay with which they were made: russet, gray, brown, yellow. Earthenware, stoneware, and creamware are just a few of the terms used to describe different types of pottery.

Every culture has fashioned some

Left: *A living room decorated with a collection of majolica plates, serving pieces, and jugs. The bright yellow walls and curtains provide the perfect background, heightening the colors of the pottery.*
Right: *A George Jones majolica oyster plate, made in mid-19th-century England, one of the many unusual pottery forms you will come across.*
Overleaf: *A closeup view of the collection. Strips of molding act as supports for the dishes. Reaching from manteltop up to the ceiling, this way of grouping the pieces is extremely eye-catching.*

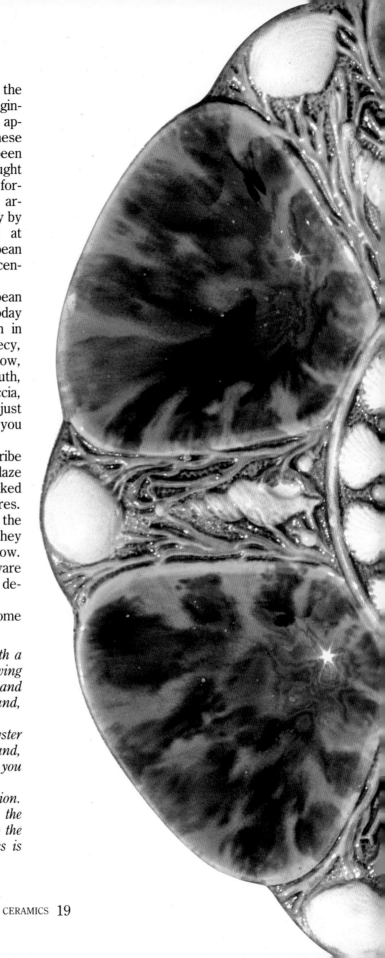

kind of pottery from the earth. The range is vast—from American Indian earthenware pots to sophisticated English Whieldon stoneware figures. Very often the type of pottery is known by the name of its maker, such as Wedgwood, or the location of its factory, such as Leeds.

Most ceramics are glazed in some way. For me, the glaze gives a piece its joyful appearance. There are many kinds of pottery that are known by the nature of their glazes. You will often come across salt-glazed pottery. The surface effect of this glaze is achieved by throwing salt directly onto the fire of the kiln. Originating in fifteenth-century Germany, this technique was used for glazing household wares, such as crocks and jugs, which today are much sought after by collectors.

In America, Rockingham, sometimes known as Bennington ware, is glazed with a manganese base that results in a rich brown color spattered over the piece, giving it the look of tortoiseshell. Italian majolica, English and Dutch delft, and French faience pottery all have a white opaque glaze made from tin oxide.

Some pottery and porcelain is intentionally left unglazed for aesthetic reasons. Porcelain of this kind is called biscuit, or bisque, while unglazed pottery is sometimes referred to as terra-cotta.

Very often you will also find enameled pieces in shops that specialize in ceramics. Quite like the glazing on a piece of pottery, enameling describes the process of firing opaque or translucent colors onto a metal surface or support, usually copper, silver, or gold. There are several kinds of enamels that you may want to know about.

With cloisonné, powdered enamel is placed into compartments formed by metal bands that become part of the design. With the champlevé technique, the powdered enamel is placed into grooves cut into the surface of the metal. Both are ancient processes. In plique-à-jour, there is no metal backing on the piece. Instead enamel fills the spaces of a delicate wireframe support resembling a miniature stained-glass window. These enameling techniques have been used to craft some of the most extraordinary treasures made by man, including drinking vessels, altar pieces, chests, and vases.

My own favorite enamels are those that were made in England during the eighteenth century in Battersea, Bilston, London, Birmingham, and Liverpool. Susan Benjamin, owner of Halcyon Days in London and author of *English Enamel Boxes from the Eighteenth to the Twentieth Centuries,* the definitive book on the subject, describes the eighteenth century as

"an age of supreme elegance when no personal belonging was considered trivial, every object—no matter how modest—was treasured."

The little enamel boxes from that era have always been irresistible to me, especially those that have enchanting sayings and scenes on them. These small keepsakes, patch boxes, and bonbonnières were also made in the shapes of animals and fruits. They were meant as little gifts then, and for those of us lucky enough to receive them now, they look very special indeed grouped on a table.

The serious study of ceramics may seem daunting and complicated, but of the things we collect, ceramics are probably the least mysterious. After all, they have been part of everyday life since we were tiny children, when perhaps our first precious baby bowl had a little bunny painted on it. What can be more familiar than something we use at every meal?

There are probably as many forms of ceramic as there are makers. Over the centuries so many wonderful shapes and decorations have evolved—tureens, teapots, urns, sugar bowls, pitchers, platters, compotes, vases, cups and saucers, candlesticks. The list goes on and on, a tribute to human inventiveness. Edith Wharton and Ogden Codman say in their book, *The Decoration of Houses,* "One of the first obligations of art is to make all useful things beautiful," and in the world of ceramics that obligation has certainly been met.

Left to right: *Whimsical Staffordshire figures beneath the gaze of a little girl of the 19th century. Although some pieces served as inkwells, or held matches or flowers, many were purely decorative and were used as fireplace ornaments.*

A salmon-pink alcove holds a lovely collection of 18th-century Chinese export armorial pieces. The topmost urn was made by Samson, about 1860.

Imaginative Chinese waterpots, crabs, and Fu dogs from the K'ang Hsi period (1662–1722) on a little table.

A graceful mantelpiece embellished with old porcelains, engravings, family photographs, and an ornate mirror.

A Dutch delft tulip vase, about 1740, made of tin-glazed earthenware. Flowers placed in each of the openings gracefully cascade from top to bottom, but even without them, the many faces and fabulous creatures make this a spectacular piece.

Intricate English pottery figures with green bocage, or foliage, were made by the Wood and Pratt families. Some pieces depict Bible scenes, others tell little stories.

Ceramics can be highly colorful and patterned, or richly decorated—trees, people, animals, buildings, landscapes, flowers—all abound. Whether hand-painted or transfer-printed, embossed, sponged, spattered, or lustered, objects on the china shelf reflect man's ingenious flair for decoration. At one time or another just about everything has been depicted on a piece of ceramic. And, in fact, lots of people collect pieces of historic blue-and-white pottery that depict buildings of architectural interest, historic events, or capture some other noteworthy subject.

My own interest in flowers found wonderful expression in all the pieces of flowery china that I've collected over the years. Nothing is nicer than going out on a bright summer day, gathering an armful of fresh flowers, and arranging them in favorite old flowered pitchers. When I'm expecting weekend guests, I fill the house with bouquets in these old jugs.

I always admire people who can be very disciplined about their collecting, concentrating on the pieces from one maker, one factory, or one period. People are often drawn to the material itself and focus on a particular type of pottery, such as American redware. Or the type of glaze may provide a focus. A geographical area could be another focus, especially in the United States and England, where facto-

Left: *Pottery translated into wood—a classical urn and flowery garlands inlaid into the surface of a Sheraton secretary.*
Above right: *A pair of 19th-century Ridgeway dishes, with auriculas, roses, and gilded grapes, complement the hand-painted foliage on an English demilune table.*
Right: *A charger with Hans Sloane botanical decoration and two gravy boats of Chelsea Red Anchor–period porcelain. The leaves, flowers, and insects are so realistically rendered that they almost look as though they have just settled on the surface. Sometimes the decoration would include small parts of the plant, inspired by detailed botanical drawings.*

Previous pages: *There are so many kinds of antique ceramics to collect.*

Left page, clockwise from above left: *Pale pastel fairings, figures sold as souvenirs at fairs in mid-19th-century England.*
Dutch delft tiles convey the spirit of country life in the mid-18th century.
A shell-shaped dish made by Wedgwood around 1860.
A collection (left) of American and English corn jugs and a mottled French Jaspé pitcher sit on a corner shelf.
Blue-and-white serving platters and other pieces surround a framed coat-of-arms from an 18th-century book.
Parian ware, first made in 1844 and used for busts, is unglazed porcelain with a marblelike matte finish very reminiscent of Wedgwood Jasperware.
A Staffordshire cottage figure on horseback on an old mantelpiece.

Right page, clockwise from above left: *A shaped plate, printed and then hand-painted with fruit and vegetables.*
A pair of early 19th-century enamel decanter labels for red and white wines.
Exotically decorated Chinese and English serving pieces and vases.
Creamware plates with bold flowers. It was first developed by Josiah Wedgwood, who called it Queen's ware in honor of Queen Charlotte of England.
A shell motif encircles an unusual Leeds pottery teapot, from about 1820.
An English dessert plate (below), painted with roses and embellished with gilt.
A small sedan chair (above) of embossed leather houses several Coalbrookdale ceramic miniatures.
A sampling of the many shapes and colors of English Staffordshire serving pieces.
Pottery and porcelain animals gather in front of a Wedgwood platter and New Hall cups and saucers.
Right: *An impressive Meissen basket-weave vase covered with extraordinarily detailed fruits and flowers. A warmly lit glass cupboard holds a collection of rare Chelsea Derby porcelain potpourri jars, made about 1769–1784.*

ries from different areas produced very distinctive wares.

While I've never been able to manage such discipline completely, I do love blue-and-white china, ranging from delftware to Chinese export. When I entertain, I like to set an entire table with my collection. I use plain white service plates and then mix all the different patterns of soup bowls, salad plates, cups and saucers, platters, and so on. The various blue-and-white pieces, pattern against pattern, always look exciting. There's no end to the diverse ways in which you can incorporate the ceramics you collect into your life and your home. They can be put to good use and enjoyed in addition to being collected. If you concentrate on a single form, you can do something as simple as group together all your cachepots or pitchers on a shelf or table. You will have created an appealing still life.

I like to move the pieces in my collection around from time to time—not just the ceramics, but other objects too. Anything that's left in one place for too long, however loved it may be, eventually becomes invisible. By moving your collection around, or putting pieces away for a while, you can make them seem new.

Not long ago, I spoke about the collector's focus with Millie Manheim of D. M. & P. Manheim Antiques, a wonderful person who has been in business for almost half a century. She exhibits each year at the Winter Antiques Show in New York City and has an unerring eye for English ceramics of particular quality. She was one of the first people I visited years ago when I became interested in the subject. We talked about the many reasons why people collect, from the scholarly and financial to the aesthetic. She told me that in her opinion the best approach to collecting is to choose "something that gives you great happiness and joy, that appeals to you, that you could live with."

Sometimes this happens almost unwittingly. I recently read of a collector of white English creamware jugs who bought

I love all types of blue-and-white pottery—it always looks fresh and crisp. In the wonderful antiques country of New England, a large serving platter beckons from an antiques shop window.
Above right: *Various shades of blue form a tabletop still life of pottery, fruit, and foliage.*
Right: *A table in a shady corner of our garden, arranged for an alfresco lunch on an old damask tablecloth.*

one piece a few years ago simply because he liked it. Soon afterward, he saw another and bought it. After his fifth purchase, he realized that he was collecting and decided he might as easily have seventy jugs as five. Since they are all off-white, they make a serene picture arranged on a pyramid of glass shelves in his living room.

When you buy pottery and porcelain, you must know what you are doing. You must be able to look at a piece intelligently and assess it with some confidence. You must gain knowledge on the subject. There are several ways of doing this.

Start by visiting antiques shops. Some of the finest and most beautiful objects can be seen close up in the shops. Take advantage of this. In addition, you will be able to talk to the person who chose the objects for the shop in the first place. A knowledgeable dealer will be happy to discuss all aspects of the pieces with you. Then go to the museums with strong collections in your area of interest. Look hard and long at what's there. Analyze what makes that piece so special.

When I asked Miss Manheim how she had gone about acquiring her great knowledge, she said that when she was just starting out, her father, who collected and sold antique ceramics, sent her with her brother to the museum, armed with notebooks. As they looked at each article in a case, they took notes on what they were seeing, jotting down the kind of handle or spout and whatever else seemed unusual or significant about the piece. Then and only then did they read the museum label and add its information to their notebooks.

While you are looking, training your eyes to see things anew, you should also be reading about ceramics. One of the things that makes this subject so interesting is the amount that you can learn about it. There are many fascinating books on ceramics. In Chapter Eight many of the shops and people that sell these books are listed.

Looking at marks is probably the first

thing that many buyers of ceramics will do. The mark can help you ascertain the manufacturer or maker of the piece and the approximate date of manufacture. But do be careful about what you decide based on marks. Once you are convinced that everything else about a piece is right, con-

The European and American delight in Chinese porcelain spawned a flourishing export trade, known as Chinese export or China trade porcelain. Millions of pieces reached the West as ballast on China clippers. Today, we especially treasure those that have survived the centuries.
Above: *A lacquered china export cabinet filled with Chinese export porcelain.*
Above left: *A closeup view of the same cabinet. Many of the shapes were made specifically to appeal to European tastes.*
Left: *A group of Famille Rose porcelain, also made for the export trade. These different forms, grouped together, serve as an unexpected centerpiece.*

sider the mark. Some pieces were given more than one mark, others were not marked at all, and some bear blatantly false imitations of the marks of very fine china. The piece may be wonderful all the

Left: A pair of 19th-century Chinese cloisonné enamel vases add balanced beauty to a tabletop.

Above: A collection of 18th-century pastel Bilston enamel boxes from Halcyon Days, one of the most appealing shops in London. Many have sayings or thoughts painted on top, such as "Love the Giver" or "A present for a friend." Others, such as those pictured here, are a bit more sophisticated. The large one in the center is a toilet box. The long tube shape is a bodkin box. Behind a very special bonbonnière painted to resemble a rose are two scent bottles.

Right: A group of desirable enamel boxes in the shapes of animals and birds, the eagle being the most rare. Scenes of nature or animals are hand-painted on the lids, either inside or out.

The sun is barely up, but the early morning rush to set up the Shaker Museum Antiques Festival is well under way. Trucks and vans arrive, bursting with antiques that will be set out in the meadow and sold that day. It's a scene that fills the imagination with anticipated delights.

same—just don't be swayed by the mark into believing it's something it's not.

In general, marks on ceramics were applied in one of four ways. They were (1) incised by a sharp tool into the soft clay, in which case the mark will have a slightly plowed-up look and a spontaneous appearance; (2) impressed in the soft clay by a stamp or seal during manufacture, resulting in a mark with a flat, neat, mechanical appearance; (3) painted on at the time of decoration, usually with the name or initial marks of the maker; or (4) printed on with engraved copper plates when the piece was decorated. Most nineteenth-century marks are printed.

In 1891 the United States required by law that all pieces of imported pottery bear the name of the country of origin on the bottom. If "England" is there, I know the piece was probably made after 1890. The law was amended in 1914 to include the words "Made in" as part of the mark. If I see "Made in England" this gives me a clue that the piece is of fairly modern origin. Since it is impossible to know all the marks, several very good sources that cover this subject are the *Encyclopedia of British Pottery and Porcelain Marks* by Geoffrey A. Godden, *Marks and Monograms on European and Oriental Pottery and Porcelain* by William Chaffers, *Handbook of Pottery and Porcelain Marks* by J. P. Cushion and W. B. Honey, and *Dictionary of Marks—Pottery and Porcelain* by Ralph M. and Terry H. Kovel (a small book that you can carry with you when you shop). No library on ceramics is complete without several of these references.

Before looking at the marks, the first thing I do when buying china is to examine its condition. If you want to have a fine collection, it should be as perfect and pristine as possible. Any imperfections in a piece will affect its value as well as its appearance. But remember, these are old pieces that have defied time by their very existence. You must expect some normal wear and tear. In fact, if a piece looks too new to you, this is a possible indication

Left: *A carton of plates, straight from the back of a van. The edges alone promise great things.*
Above: *The line forms early at the gate. Some shows now have early admission fees, which enable you to be admitted several hours before the show opens to the public.*
Below: *A graceful ironstone mark on the base of a 19th-century piece. W. Baker & Company was in business in England from 1839 to 1932.*

that it is not what it should be.

When you inspect a piece, look especially at the bottom, to see if there is wear. There should be little scratches where the piece was picked up and put down. This is normal on any antique piece. Next, look carefully for things that don't constitute normal wear. Feel with your fingers along the edges for chips that may not be obvious to the eye. Also run your fingers over the entire surface, feeling for hairline cracks.

Always ask a dealer if he knows whether a piece has been repaired or restored. Look very carefully yourself. Some restoration that is done today is very difficult to spot. I've seen wary collectors and dealers at antiques shows using ultraviolet lights to help them spot signs of old repair. The more aware you are, the more educated your eye becomes and the better you see details that once were overlooked.

Although I do think the things that you buy should be just as pristine as possible, there are some exceptions to this. If a piece is very rare, something you've spent years searching for, then it would be silly not to buy it just because it isn't perfect. Rarity offsets condition in this case.

Another factor is less tangible. Emotions, like antiques, are not an exact science. If you love something, you should buy it. I will very often find a plate or a jug that, although broken, gives me great joy. It may be very affordable and so I buy it. It may have a crude Victorian staple repair that says to me that someone cared enough about it to repair and preserve it.

Historical blue-and-white Staffordshire pottery set out in early morning. Dinner and dessert plates, covered sugar bowls, creamer, and teapot are characterized by the deep, distinctive blue color. The plates, decorated with scenes commemorating places and historic events, looking so attractive here, would look even more wonderful grouped on a dark wood sideboard.

Frog Alley
Tag
Sale
←

Memories from a day at the Shaker Museum Antiques Festival.

Above: *Before the big rush, a quilt dealer, who is here every year, staves off the early morning chill with a welcome cup of coffee.*

Left: *We stretch the excitement of the day by stopping at tag and yard sales to and from the show. There are always bargains and surprises to be found—you never know what you will discover.*

Below: *A typical scene of dealers setting up for the show, with some early lookers, too.*

One old jug I have is repaired in this way. It will not hold water, so I fill it with dried flowers and turn its staple side to the wall. I've had so many compliments on it, and only I know its secret.

Searching for antiques is always exciting. I love the whole process of looking, examining, comparing, asking questions. Nothing, however, is more exciting than the anticipation of an outdoor antiques market in the country, where I know I will always find something to add to my collection of blue and white china. When I can smell the first breath of spring in the air, I know it's time to start poring over the antiques newspapers and tearing out lists of the antiques shows. The season for me starts in May with the Brimfield, Massachusetts, show, one of the largest in the northeast. It ends in late summer with one of my favorites, The One Day Rural Original Flea Market, in Salisbury, Connecticut. There is a special list of some of my other favorite antiques shows in Chapter Eight.

A midsummer focal point is always the Shaker Museum Antiques Festival in Old Chatham, New York, held on the grounds of the Shaker Museum. We make a family outing of it every year, getting up at dawn, when the air is so fresh and clean. We pack a picnic lunch, everybody piles into the van, and we're off. Just getting to and from there is part of the adventure. The countryside is beautiful and there are yard and barn sales all along the way. We stop every five minutes, to look and buy. We also hit every fresh vegetable market and fruit stand on the way and often arrive in Old Chatham with our van already half filled.

My nieces and nephews look forward to it with as much eagerness as I do. Several are starting to collect, and while one searches out old postcards, another looks for antique penknives. My niece enjoys hunting for miniature china for her dollhouse. There's something for everyone. Once we've gathered our treasures and had lunch under some shady tree, we visit

My Jasperware jug showing its old Victorian staple repairs (left) *and* (right) *filled with a bouquet of dried flowers from the garden, repaired side to the wall. Early restorations like this sometimes did more damage than good.*

the museum, which is just lovely and adds another dimension to the day.

All summer long, antiques shows give us a wonderful excuse to travel, to leave our gardening chores and paperwork for the weekend. Mel and I both love old country inns and can always find some wonderful place to stay. We love discovering new restaurants and scan our guidebooks for those nearby. There are always new museums, historical societies, or old houses to explore.

Hunting for antiques also gives travel abroad a focus. We try to coordinate trips to England with the Grosvenor House Antique Show if we can. A trip to Florence or Paris is always extra special if the Biennale is held that year, and visiting the châteaus in France can be coordinated with special outdoor markets and antiques shops in the towns in between. Whether at home or abroad, I always know that I will find some treasure or learn something that day.

I also learn so much at country markets. The atmosphere is relaxed and everything is accessible. Many of the oldest, most interesting dealers in this country are at the same shows year after year. These people are continually searching for new merchandise and their booths are

Above left: *The homey appeal of English jugs and food pots offering clotted cream, toiletries, and other patented preparations. Their decoration, consisting mostly of different sized letters and typefaces, has a very graphic beauty.*

Above right: *Part of my white ironstone collection in glass-fronted kitchen cupboards, where individual pieces can easily be found and always be enjoyed. Ironstone was patented in 1813 by Charles James Mason and was produced in America and England. One rarely sees the white ironstone in England now as most of it was exported to this country between 1845 and 1880.*

filled with items found perhaps in the attic of an old farmhouse or in a barn. They will often research these pieces and bring them to the market that same weekend. Generally all are friendly, happy to be out in the open air and to share what they know. I have learned so much about pottery at these shows. I always ask for the

story behind the piece. Where was it made, how old do they think it is, what history does it have—that kind of thing. I've made many friends this way, and though I may see them only once a year, it's always a great pleasure when I do.

When we turn the car homeward, we are all feeling the pleasant glow of a day well spent. We've met new friends and old and connected to the stream of history as we looked at so many beautiful objects from the past. Germain Seligman, whose father was a famous art dealer in turn-of-the-century Paris, wrote in his book, *Merchants of Art,* that art and antiques are "a joy to be shared by all who are willing to see and to feel, a great international tongue by which men can speak and be thrilled across the centuries and across the world." Whether you are drawn to exquisite pieces of porcelain or humble pottery jugs or to an entirely different group of antiques, they all have an eloquence that speaks to us from another time.

Caring for Ceramics

I have confessed to a weakness for mended pieces of beautiful old china. Their survival reflects the love and respect of their owners down through the years. However, it is still far better to prevent breakage from occurring in the first place. Here are some tips for handling, cleaning, and storing your ceramics.

- Always approach cleaning, dusting, or washing ceramics very carefully. Make sure you will have plenty of time to tackle the project. Do not be in a rush.

- As a precaution, cover your work area with soft padding—a terry-cloth towel or several layers of paper toweling will do. If you drop anything, it will land on a cushioned surface and be less likely to break.

- For dusting decorative ceramics—especially figurines and other sculpted pieces—use a soft, thick watercolor brush reserved for that job alone.

- Don't overdo washing your delicate ceramic pieces. In most cases, a gentle once-over with a damp cotton ball will suffice. Never submerge any restored or repaired ceramics in water. Enamel or porous objects should never be washed. When in doubt, don't.

- If a total wash is in order, then you must be sure to line the sink—bottom and sides—with a rubber pad or towels. Or have a separate plastic bowl set aside for this job. Use lukewarm soapy water (I use a mild detergent such as Ivory liquid). Avoid any extremes of water temperature, which may lead to cracking of fragile pieces. Dip the object in and gently wipe it off.

- If the object has protrusions—leaves, flower petals, fingers—never use a cloth for the wash. To get around these vulnerable places, use a soft toothbrush or cotton swab and gently brush away the dirt. Never soak.

- Spreading paper towels under it, let the piece air-dry in a safe place, where it will not be disturbed until it is ready to be put away.

- Never pick up a piece of ceramic by a spout, rim, lid, or handle. Lift by the biggest area and always use two hands, one to lift and the other to support the object. When moving ceramics from one place to another, never stack or carry more than one piece at a time. It's far safer to make two trips.

- When you're storing ceramics, always make sure there is adequate space. Never crowd too many things on a shelf. Never let one piece touch or lean on another. It helps to store the big things in the back, the smaller things in front.

- Always position the ceramics well away from the edge. If there are vibrations in the building—from nearby construction, for example—an object could just walk right off the shelf.

- Never stack one thing inside of another. You can easily be tempted to do this, especially if you're living in an apartment and trying to save space. If you must, then line the larger object with felt or newspaper. Or wrap the smaller object before putting it inside the larger one. Even with this precaution, you're always running the risk that you're not going to remember that something is there.

- Plates are one thing you must stack to store. Never stack them too high. Put a piece of felt or paper between the plates to protect them from scratching each other. I cut the pieces of felt to size so the cupboard looks neat and I can see the plates. This task may sound tedious, but you can reuse the felt or paper for years to come. Ready-cut felt or quilted disks are also sold at many houseware stores.

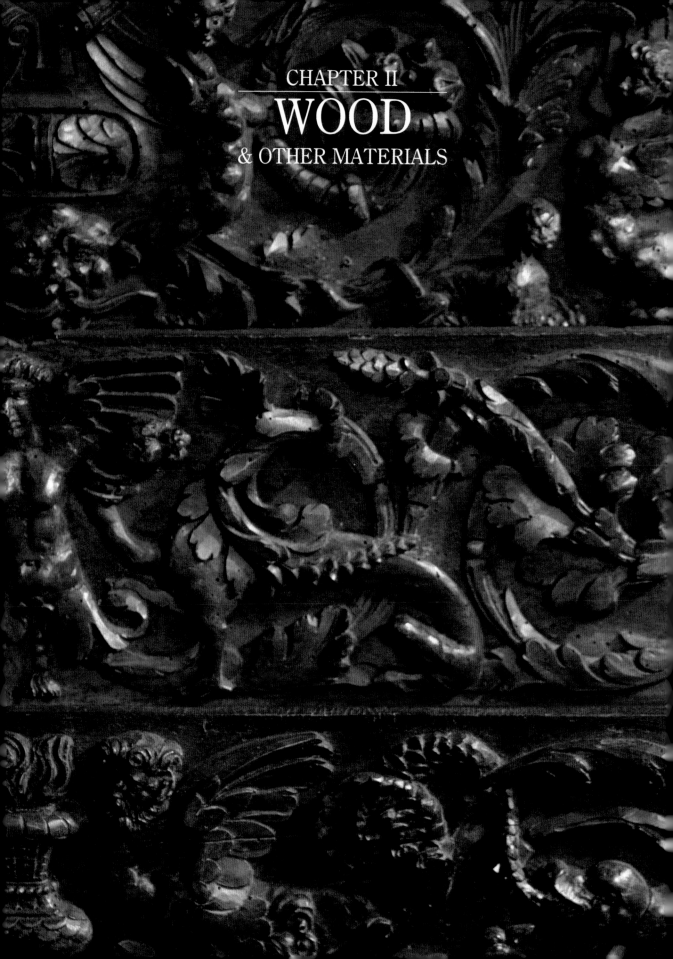

CHAPTER II
WOOD
& OTHER MATERIALS

The first antique I ever bought was a pincushion-topped wood sewing box. Not only was it useful, but it reminded me of the generations of American women who relied on their wits and their needles to produce the extraordinary quilts and samplers that I love. Many people think of such antique boxes as functional and commonplace. But in *Neat and Tidy,* a charming and informative book on the subject that has become almost a classic, Nina Fletcher Little, the American decorative arts expert, writes that these functional containers were "among the truly cherished possessions of most American families."

From that first sewing box I went on to collect boxes of all sorts—lap desks, jewelry boxes, bonbonnières, snuffboxes, workboxes, pillboxes, and hatboxes. Over the years I've used them in many different ways in my home. They take up little space while holding and hiding all sorts of things. They hold letters, keep rubber bands handy, store a button collection, hide my hairpins. Occasionally, they've even been used for their original purpose, as in the case of my sewing box. Whether they are stacked on the floor or tucked into a bookshelf, they lend a particular style to a room.

Sitting on a table, these boxes impart a warmth and mellowness that only come from polished wood. One of its most ap-

Previous page: *A detail of 16th-century Italian and 17th-century Dutch panels, alive with fabulous carved creatures and foliage.*
Above: *Faux marble finishes cover the top of a Regency tripod table from about 1810.*
Right: *Lyrical wood fragments and carved reference pieces, used as guides when restoring, hang on a wall at Carvers and Guilders, restorers, in London.*

A teak Indian temple carving serves as a backdrop for a collection of wood objects, including English oak candlesticks, Russian burlwood bud vases, shoe-shaped snuffboxes, a large burl box, and a paper knife, all from the 19th century.

pealing aspects is the glow, or surface quality—what is called patina. Whether we are talking about a tea caddy or a desk, the patina adds immeasurably to its worth in many ways. It is acquired over years of loving use and care.

In *American Treasure Hunt,* Harold Sack describes his father, Israel Sack, one of America's most notable antiques dealers (whose store, Israel Sack, Inc., is still in New York City), trying to dissuade a client from refinishing a piece of furniture. He said, "You see that hard wood with its patina? That took at least a hundred and fifty years of natural wear, of people living with it, and using it every day, to get that beautiful patina. Now if you take that finish and plane it, and scrape it, . . . believe me, neither you nor your children, nor your grandchildren, will live to see that patina grow back again."

Other experts, such as Wallace Nutting, who wrote *Furniture Treasury* in 1933, a classic book on the design and structure of American furniture, feel that anything marred should be refinished. If

Above: *Four 18th-century blacka-moors, supporting jardinières, greet visitors at the entrance to the Partridge Fine Art Gallery, where you can find the finest in English and French furniture. I always stop in to look when I'm in London.*
Right: *Wood is often embellished with other materials. The Georgian footed boxes are covered in rich leather and ornamented with feet, handles, and locks in ormolu. An early 19th-century gilt wood jardinière is festooned with carved swags.*

Left: *An inlaid zebrawood card table holding an assortment of handsome wood, tortoise, and penwork boxes.* Below: *One of a pair of English Georgian mahogany knife boxes with monogrammed silver mounts and delicate satinwood inlay.*

the patina has already been damaged by neglect or abuse, refinishing will at least restore the original beauty of the surface when new. Both schools of thought recognize the importance of patina.

It is almost impossible to talk about wood without discussing furniture. By looking at and studying furniture, you will learn about the small objects that were also made from wood. Treen is a word used to describe the small everyday wooden objects that were hand-carved or turned on lathes. From the seventeenth century on, simple household goods such as wooden spoons, goblets, trenchers, and bowls were made in this way. The first settlers in America may not have brought much fine silver or china, but they did have some of these beautifully made wood objects, which are now rare and sought after. Today the term treen is also used much more broadly to describe any small wooden collectors' pieces.

If you want to learn about wood, it is important to recognize the kind of wood used in making the objects. Identifying base woods can help you to tell when a piece was made. Mahogany, for example, was the favorite choice of American cabinetmakers from about 1740 to 1840. In England, oak was the prime wood of the sixteenth and seventeenth centuries.

Each kind of wood—from ash to zebrawood—has its own special characteristics. Some, such as mahogany and oak, are best suited to the broad strokes of large pieces, while others, such as pear, come to life when finely carved. There are

Small boxes and other wood objects are fun to collect, easy to display, and take up just a little bit of space, an important consideration for many of us.

Above left: *Several tea caddies from the 18th century, including a pear-shaped one made of fruitwood. Except for the scallop, which is pewter, the shells are the real thing, transformed into snuffboxes with silver and brass mounts.*

Above center: *An English fire fan made of papier-mâché and hand-painted with a genre scene against a plaid background. Papier-mâché, made from pulped paper, was then lacquered and used to make decorative objects, such as trays, cachepots, and boxes. It was popular in the 18th and 19th centuries.*

Above right: *A collection of tartanware,* including boxes, napkin rings, an hourglass and cribbage board, sewing accessories, a jackknife, and letter opener. These little souvenirs, given as gifts, were popular in England during Queen Victoria's reign, 1837–1901. Each object is wood, covered in a different tartan plaid paper.

Below, left and center: *Scenes of sunny Brighton, a popular Regency and Victorian vacation spot, are painted or drawn in pen and ink on these paper-covered wood objects. Workboxes, candlestands, trays, game boards, and even a sewing bird pincushion (center) would bring back memories of pleasant days by the sea.*

Below: *A pack of delightful dogs, all carved in wood, rest contentedly on a papier-mâché tray. Most of these are boxes, although one holds a pen in his mouth.*

also woods such as fruitwoods, that are so rare and costly that they must be used sparingly, in combination with more economical base ones. It is important to recognize the way in which these woods are applied to other woods.

A *veneer* is a very thin sheet of fine wood that is bonded to the surface of another, coarser wood. Veneer can be all of one wood or of several woods combined.

In *marquetry* thin pieces of rare, colorful woods are arranged in a decorative pattern and applied as a veneer to the surface of a piece. Old marquetry designs were often geometric, but there are extraordinary bouquets of flowers, musical instruments, and other subjects that have been rendered this way in wood.

In *parquetry,* which is used for floors, woods of the same colors are arranged in a mosaic or other pattern that, like marquetry, completely covers the base wood.

Inlay is another way of decorating the surface of an object. Precious woods or other materials such as mother-of-pearl and ivory are cut into small pieces and fitted right into the base wood in a pattern to form a single, smooth surface.

Design and craftsmanship are the first things one should consider when looking at an object or furniture. When a piece is faultlessly made and has good scale and proportion, it possesses an unmistakable integrity. Many of the finest were made by a handful of craftsmen and cabinetmakers. This is why there is so much emphasis on names—Thomas Sheraton, Robert Adam, John Goddard, Thomas Affleck, Jean Henri Riesener, Jean François Oeben, Duncan Phyfe, Georges Jacob, and others. Their names are closely associated with the very best quality. While few of us will ever be able to acquire anything of this rarity for our homes today, it is still worthwhile to know their work.

By studying exquisitely made pieces, you come to appreciate and learn about very fine craftsmanship, where the craftsperson really reached within to produce

Left: *The warmth of an ash Biedermeier secretary, about 1820, is enhanced by the collection of objects on it. Russian burlwood cigarette cases are along one side and blue john goblets on the other.*
Above: *A dressing stand and very unusual wood towel rack, from about 1840, fit snugly into the screened dressing area of a bedroom filled with 18th- and 19th-century silk fabrics.*
Overleaf: *A beautifully balanced sitting room—elegant, yet relaxed and welcoming. Well-loved objects collected over a lifetime blend comfortably with new items that are added from time to time.*

something very special. Grinling Gibbons, England's finest wood-carver, once simulated a piece of lace in carved wood, for example, just to prove it could be done.

Knowing the cabinetmakers and the periods in which they worked is very important. Major periods usually bear a political designation, such as Empire or Federal; the name of a reigning house, such as Tudor or Elizabethan; or the name of a monarch, such as Queen Anne or Louis XIV. Periods are simply a measure of time, of the moment in history during which certain pieces were made. Each country has its own breakdown of periods.

Styles are usually associated with specific craftspeople or designers working within the various periods. In England, for example, Thomas Chippendale, the famous furniture maker, was at work during the Georgian period. In France, André-Charles Boulle, an *ébéniste,* was working in the Louis XIV period. Duncan Phyfe, a New York cabinetmaker, worked during the American Federal period.

There are many excellent books on antique furniture, including *Fine Points of Furniture* by Albert Sack, on American objects, and *The Dictionary of English Furniture* by Percy Macquoid and Ralph Edwards. Remember that young America was influenced by what happened in Europe, particularly England, and it usually took about ten years for developments there to be felt in the New World.

Doing your homework is essential if

Left: *A miniature portrait cabinet swings open to reveal a large collection of tiny portraits that were gathered together in the early 18th century by one member of the family. The mutton-fat jade below was collected by another family member at a later time.*
Right, above and center: *Painted on ivory, each miniature is a little biography of someone who lived long ago.*
Right: *Some miniatures, like this charming one of a child, were set into the tops of boxes.*

A corner of Joanna Booth's shop in London, as inviting as a garden bower. A hound chases a hare on a carved 14th-century oak chimney beam. Flora and fauna are woven into Flemish and French tapestries from the 16th and 17th centuries and are carved into wood fragments.
Right: Tortoiseshell etuis, needle boxes, and a workbox surrounded by needlework and tapestry flowers.

you are buying antique furniture today. Not only has it become expensive, but it is something that you will be living with intimately, looking at every single day. If you buy wisely and well, you will love every minute of sitting in that antique wing chair, sleeping in that old sleigh bed, or eating at that splendid gateleg table.

Alastair Stair, whose father founded Stair and Andrew in England in 1912 and who opened Stair and Company in New York City in 1935, told me about a young couple who came to him years ago. The husband was a schoolteacher and they had a limited budget. They made an arrangement to buy furniture gradually, giving Mr. Stair a check every month for a small amount. They now have a collection worth many times their initial investment. That may no longer be possible, but if you buy, "buy the best, the best you can afford," as Mr. Stair recommends, and you will never be disappointed. Your own research and a knowledgeable dealer will help you to choose quality.

Another benefit of buying fine furniture and wood objects is that they almost always hold their value. For example, if you are just starting out, living in a small apartment perhaps, you may buy a small table for the breakfast nook. Later, when your taste or circumstances change—perhaps the family expands or you move to a

house—you can often sell it back to the store you bought it from and buy a larger table. Or you can sell it at auction. If you bought well in the first place, the piece will have an intrinsic worth.

Browsing in antiques shops is one of my favorite pastimes. Whenever I'm in a new place, one of the first things I do is look in the Yellow Pages under "Antiques." Antiques shops are usually clustered. In Boston, for example, there are many on Charles Street, and in Philadelphia, on Pine Street. I always call a few to see what their hours are, and then I plan my day. In New York City, shops are grouped in many locations, from the eclectic shops in Greenwich Village to Fifty-seventh Street, where some of the oldest shops are located, to upper Madison Avenue, an area of new antiques surprises.

When I go abroad, I do the same thing. I am still collecting boxes, and London is where I have found some of the best ones. I began my collection there with the purchase of a particularly beautiful fruitwood tea caddy inlaid with a shell motif. On my first morning in London, I indulge myself with a walk down Bond Street, which hasn't changed much since the days when Henry James's prince in *The Golden Bowl* strolled along it. I look in at Sotheby's to see what's doing and then cross the street to Partridge's, which is filled

with the dignified elegance of the past. I end up at the Ritz for tea, my head filled with all the beautiful things I've seen. There's Kensington Church Street, Fulham Road, Mount Street, and many more, for London is an antiques lover's paradise. As often as I visit this city, I always find new shops mixed in with the old familiar ones. I have listed some of both for you in Chapter Eight.

Being aware of the condition of the wood helps you to spot some of the "pitfalls for collectors," as Wallace Nutting calls them. Wooden furniture and items can be made up of fragments rescued from other pieces. For example, on a table, a new top may have been added to an old table base. A chair may have one or more replacement legs or feet. The top section of a highboy may not match the bottom. The two original parts became separated at some point and reattached to other partners, becoming what are known as "married" pieces. These alterations may have occurred at any time during the life of a piece for any number of reasons. If you know your woods, periods, styles, and construction, very likely you will be able to recognize such adaptations, repairs, and restorations.

You also must examine each object carefully. If you are buying a set of something—chairs, for example—spend time examining each one. It is not unusual for one or two chairs in a set to be reproductions, made to round out the number or to replace damaged chairs. There's really

Assortments of small objects made of natural materials always look great arranged on tabletops.

Left to right: *A square box and oblong spectacle case in pale shagreen that complements the bronze stand and the Italian watercolor landscape behind.*

Horn beakers with silver mounts made in the 19th century join little boxes and trays on an elaborately painted 18th-century Chinese export tray at Charlotte Moss in New York City.

Objects of piqué—tortoiseshell inlaid with gold or silver—surrounding and atop a Victorian miniature inlaid table. The intricacy and craftsmanship of pieces like this, so delicately decorated with tiny figures and flowers, is extraordinary.

A 19th-century French desk ensemble made of polished malachite. This green stone with black veining is found mostly in Russia and was often used by Fabergé to make the most magnificent objects.

Late 19th-century vases and paperweights sculpted from agate.

Overleaf: *Baskets filled with fabrics, trimmings, shells, dried flowers, and other treasures climb a staircase.*

nothing wrong with reproductions—some are very well made indeed. But you should check whether a piece is an original or not before you buy it.

Very often, when I'm wandering in antiques shops, I find decorative objects made of other natural materials. Most are familiar and I will list and define them here.

• *Ivory* is derived from the tusks of elephants or other tusked animals. It is a hard, creamy-white dentine substance that was used to make many decorative objects in the past—games and buttons, for example. Before photography, miniature portraits were painted on ivory and worn or carried by loved ones.

• *Tortoiseshell* is quite simply the shell of the turtle. The finest came from the island of Coiba in the Pacific. It was used as an inlay material and also to fashion combs, boxes, paper knives, fans, and other delicate objects.

• *Horn* is the bony appendage of many animals, such as elk, deer, and antelope. Horns, which were easily hollowed, have been used for various forms, such as beakers and snuffboxes.

• *Shagreen* is the rough skin usually of sharks and rays, which was frequently dyed green. It was used in the 1700s and became popular again in the 1920s and '30s for desk accessories.

• *Jade* is a term used to describe two minerals: nephrite and jadeite. Of the two, nephrite is the more desirable. It is usually of a subdued green color, but there is also a "mutton-fat" white jade that is very choice. Jadeite is usually more vividly colored. Jade objects are especially associated with the Orient.

• *Malachite*, *agate*, and *marble* are also minerals. They were carved and polished until they glowed with a cool beauty and were often fashioned into inkwells, pen holders, cups, and miniatures of ancient monuments.

There are some things you should be aware of. Because of the increasing numbers of wildlife species that are endangered today, there are ever-changing laws controlling the importation of some of these materials—tortoiseshell and ivory, for example—into our country. Quite rightly, the importation of contemporary objects made of these materials is becoming more and more restricted. And even though antique objects were made at least a hundred years ago, before these animals were endangered, I would still suggest a call to the U.S. Fish and Wildlife Service for the latest information on bringing these things through customs.

Most of these objects are in some way functional and can add style to the most ordinary setting or activity. I keep a horn cup filled with pencils by the telephone, for example, and another sits on my bedside table. Cigarette boxes become useful again when filled with potpourri or candies, and using an old letter opener brightens a mundane task.

Rooms can also be lightened and humanized with old baskets. They can be coiled or woven, made from every imaginable plant and other substances as well —tree bark, wood splints, pine needles, willows, reeds, raffia. Basketry is an art in which the human hand excels. I especially love the simple, finely wrought baskets fashioned by the Shakers, who appreciated the value of all growing things and made baskets from materials many considered useless. "The ability to look at

Clockwise from upper left: *A painted enamel basket, about 1890, tied shut with old ribbon, on a cast-iron garden bench at Colefax and Fowler, London.*
A flat apple-drying basket on the wall above a row of 19th-century American baskets.
Old American gardening baskets and English trugs are indoors, protected from the elements when not in use.
New England baskets fill a painted Connecticut cupboard. The carved wooden busts have faux marble bases and sit on an early 19th-century American butterfly leaf table with a pine top and maple base.

anything and dream up a use for it takes considerable imagination and effort," writes June Sprigg, in *By Shaker Hands,* her lovely book on Shaker arts. "But how much easier it is when you're convinced that even a weed has a definite purpose since God saw it fit to put on earth."

There is no end to the ways in which you can use baskets. In fact, there isn't a room in the house where I don't have a basket. The most precious little ones sit on shelves—works of art in their own right. In the kitchen, sturdier ones hang from the ceiling on hooks. But in truth, they are wonderful containers for anything and everything. Nothing looks prettier than a small basket lined with a damask napkin and filled with hot muffins. In the bedroom, a basket on a desk holds letters. A big one beside a favorite armchair is a perfect place for magazines. They can be filled with kindling or pinecones beside the fireplace. They keep wool or needlework projects handy. And of course, as many of you know, I put potpourri in some of mine.

Baskets, like anything made of wood or plant fibers, make a room seem more friendly, cozy, and inviting. And it is in these livable rooms in which we are most comfortable and happy. The aesthetics of wood and the importance of conservation have been written about very sensitively by Eric Sloane in his many valuable and instructive books. As he says in *A Reverence for Wood,* "Gentle to the touch, exquisite to contemplate, tractable in creative hands, stronger by weight than iron, wood was, as William Penn had said, 'A substance with a soul.' "

Left: *An eye-catching stack of late 19th-century American work and storage boxes. Meticulously painted to resemble wood grain, and decorated, each one probably has a story to tell about the tools or supplies it once held.*
Right: *A line of English pine bread boards. Sometimes carved with wheat motifs or the word* bread, *they can be used to serve cheeses or dessert loaves.*

A Dutch flagon or jug, probably a trade sign, on display. It is made of a piece of solid wood and, with its old green paint flaking off, has a simple dignity. Beside it, a pale wood charger shows the appealing wear of many years of use.

Caring for Wood & Other Materials

Beautiful old woods glow with a warmth that is very special. The beauty of antique boxes that have been waxed and tended carefully reflects loving care by many people over the years. Here are some tips for keeping your wood antiques in the best possible condition.

- Boxes and other little wood antiques should be dusted very lightly with a soft, dry brush or small dust rag. I prefer not to use a dust rag, since loose threads can catch on pieces of veneer or marquetry, pulling them off. Be very careful if you do.

- Never use anything that has a rough texture to it—it might actually scratch the wood you are trying to preserve. And that means avoid feather dusters too. Broken feathers are like little scratchy sticks that will mar the surface.

- Remember to take the dust off the piece entirely. This may sound silly, but a lot of times, when an object has wax on it, you just move the dust around.

- Always use a good-quality paste wax to wax the wood. I like to use beeswax from Scotland or England. Just apply a little at a time, rubbing softly following the grain of the wood, to build up the deep layered finish your wood deserves. The patina on a wood object or piece of furniture is very important and must be nurtured.

- Use a very soft cloth for waxing. Cheesecloth is excellent. Do not overdo the amount of wax you use. Spread on a thin, even coat and rub evenly and gently to bring up a high polish. You want to build up a good finish with wax, one that will seal and protect the wood underneath.

- Be very gentle when waxing. If a piece of veneer or inlay comes loose, save it. Such pieces are irreplaceable; substitutes are impossible to find. The pieces should be tucked away in a safe place, then brought to a furniture or wood expert to restore. Don't attempt to glue them back or to make the repairs yourself.

- Many wood antiques have some kind of metal ornamentation—brass keyholes or knobs, ormolu, or other decoration. These bits of metal should not be polished with any metal-cleaning product. By polishing the metal, you take a chance on damaging the wood underneath. Instead you should just dust them carefully several times a year.

- If your house or apartment is especially dry in winter, you should use a humidifier. Wood responds to changes in temperature and humidity. It swells or shrinks and can warp or split. So try to avoid extremes in temperature and make sure that your wood objects do not dry out or become too damp. In the old days, dealers who brought a shipment in from Britain or Europe put their new stock in a warehouse for a year to let it get used to our drier climate. Nowadays, economics preclude this and pieces go right to the showroom, so in most cases a humidifier is a must.

- In the case of spills, stains, or serious scratches, I prefer not to use homemade remedies, and instead always call a good wood restorer to assess and repair the damage.

- Jade, ivory, horn, and marble should be lightly dusted with a soft brush or dry, soft cloth. Keep these objects out of direct sunlight, since they may dry out and become brittle. Always handle these objects with care when moving them.

In her spirited memoir *Blackberry Winter* Margaret Mead, the noted anthropologist, talks about the things that mattered to her as a child. She writes, "There were treasures on Mother's dressing table . . . a Wedgwood pin dish, a little porcelain Mary and her lamb, the pale green, flowered top of a rose bowl that had broken, and Mother's silver-backed comb and brush and mirror. All these things held meaning for me. Each was—and still is—capable of evoking a rush of memories."

Because of the memories they evoke for us, I think antique silver objects are often among our most treasured possessions. Handed down from one generation to the next, they become one of the threads in a family's history. A parent's baby mug engraved with name and date or a great-grandmother's set of silver teaspoons become precious keepsakes.

They are also part of everyday living and of special celebrations—the festive punch bowl and its generous ladle at Christmastime, the gleaming silver coffee urn on the sideboard at an anniversary dinner, the simple salt and pepper shakers on the dining table at every meal. These pieces travel with us through our lives, growing older with a special grace.

Over the centuries, many different forms have been rendered in silver, from the commonplace to the unusual—flatware and serving pieces, toast racks, decanter labels, tankards, sauceboats, tea and chocolate pots, epergnes, and spice boxes. Set on a shelf or on a beautifully laid table, old silver pieces add vitality to a room, reflecting light and shadow on their glittering, lustrous surfaces.

Mixing patterns of flatware when setting the table is both unusual and decorative. You can assemble your own set of old silver with spoons, knives, forks, and serving pieces that coordinate but do not match or with place settings, each in a different pattern. In this way you also take advantage of the market, where there is often an abundance of one form but not others in the same pattern or only a few place settings in a pattern. A collection of silver salt and pepper shakers, a different set for each place, can also be assembled this way.

I like to use a pitcher to serve water at each meal. Nothing looks lovelier than the silver beaded with moisture as we sit down to dinner. I also use it for serving wine, milk, or other drinks.

Silver utensils such as ice tongs and buckets, olive jars, trays, little dishes, and champagne icers complement glass decanters and glasses on a sideboard. Tea implements can also be the focus of a collection—caddies, strainers, caddy spoons, and the many other pieces that reflect the ritual of afternoon tea. A dressing table looks especially interesting when furnished with mixed patterns of silver-backed brushes and mirrors, powder jars, and perfume bottles. Silver objects transform a desktop and intensify the glow of the wood. Silver cups can hold pencils and scissors, and a toast rack is perfect for letters awaiting an answer.

Not as costly as gold, silver is accessible to most of us. Whether you are looking for small pieces or more important historic articles, when you buy silver there are several things to consider.

I was talking about old silver with Edward Munves, the dynamic president of James Robinson in New York, founded by

Previous page: *French 19th-century chocolate pots, coffeepots, teapots, and ewers, all ornamented with repoussé decoration and arranged on a shelf in front of a set of service plates.*

Above left: *One of four silver corners made by Tiffany and Company, New York, about 1890, for a very elegant desk blotter. Flowers, ferns, and foliage, popular themes at the turn of the century, are hammered up in high relief.*

Right: *An oval 19th-century frame by Kirk and Sons of Baltimore sits atop an early French damask cloth.*

his uncle in 1912. Mr. Munves has an enthusiasm that is infectious. I asked him how he would approach buying and collecting silver. He told me that when he studies a piece there are three criteria that must be met. "It must have good design, fine craftsmanship, and be in excellent condition. The design may be exquisite, but when you examine the piece closely, you may find that it is not finished well. Or it may have both great design and craftsmanship, but show signs that through the years people have abused it—a coat of arms may have been erased, a cover replaced, a candlestick column broken.

"Once a piece meets all three criteria, then and only then do labels enter in —age, maker's name, important historical connections, rarity of form or of type, and anything else that makes the piece special, affecting its value and price. My mind is looking and weighing and judging all of these criteria at the same time."

In buying silver you look first for quality. Age alone or a famous maker's name is not enough to make an object really desirable. Mr. Munves says, "If you can't afford the Georgian, try the Victorian. If you can't afford that, try the Edwardian. One can always find marvelous pieces. It just needs an open mind to go out and discover them. If you are really serious about owning wonderful silver, buy great late things rather than ordinary or bad early things. Some good objects were made in every period."

Many times you come upon a piece about which you have only very sketchy

Clockwise from top: *A dressing table with old and new silver powder and trinket boxes and other objects, including a papier-mâché jewelry box.*
A traveling dressing case made in London in 1843 and fitted with silver and cut-glass toilet accessories.
English frames, card cases, vanity jars, and scent bottles from the 19th century sparkle on the mirrorlike surface of a polished wood table.

On my dressing table are objects that belonged to my mother and grand-mother. Dried flowers fill an American cut-glass decanter. Touches of lace, ribbon, and family photographs complete the picture.

information, if any. Doing research is part of the fun of living with antiques. You may have chanced upon something very special. When I was discussing this with Mr. Munves, he said, "It is better to disprove than prove a piece in order to validate it. If you can find all the things that are wrong with it and eliminate them one by one, eventually you can be confident that the piece is right."

While we are on the subject of buying, there are some other considerations. When I am buying any antique, I always make sure to get a sales receipt that gives details about the purchase—a description of the item, its price, the maker's name if known, the date when it was made, its provenance, if known, and notes on any restoration that has been done to the piece. This record is very helpful to have for insurance and appraisal purposes and also if something about the piece bothers you later.

When buying silver, look at the object carefully. If it looks worn out, you probably shouldn't buy it. Silver should be in pristine condition, especially since it is something that is used often. Look at the area where initials or a crest might have been. People occasionally try to remove these, and such tampering affects the aesthetics, if not the value, of the article.

Also look for hallmarks, which are usually grouped together, either on the bottom or in an inconspicuous place near an edge. Make certain that they are original to the piece. Occasionally you may see very old or desirable hallmarks that have been let in to a later object, and the seam will show when the piece is tarnished. With something designed to hold liquid—teapots, coffeepots, and pitchers—you can sometimes spot signs of damage by holding the piece up to the light and looking inside. It can always be repaired, but you should know it needs repair before you buy it. Also take care that the piece is all original and does not have a handle or finial from something else soldered on.

Left: *English presentation silver snuffboxes and vinaigrettes, dating from 1769 to 1823, and engraved with inscriptions voicing gratitude or respect.*

Below far left: *A tray of Victorian card cases, both American and English, which held the finely embossed visiting cards that were an important part of one's daily social rounds.*

Below left: *Silver vinaigrettes, made about 1820, each an inch long, that once held tiny sponges soaked in scented vinegars. Vapors escaped through the pierced silver grill to ward off fainting spells.*

Above: *Barry Witmond, one of London's fine restorers, uses an ivory mallet to remove a bruise from a piece of old silver.*

Below: *Hallmarks on the bottom of an English porringer, which show that the piece is silver. It was made in London in 1686 by a maker whose initials were DG.*

And what about replating? People ask about this all the time. Some experts argue that it should never be done, others say by all means replate tired silver. My own feeling is that each piece sets its own rule. I don't mind when silver shows use. Use means that people have loved an object; it has been part of their lives. I would not replate this piece. However, if you have something that is in bad condition, isn't very special, something functional that you want to enjoy, then go ahead. If you are not sure what to do, take it to a silver conservator before doing anything.

What we think of as solid or sterling silver is not pure silver. Silver alone, like gold, is too soft to withstand general use. Both metals must be alloyed with small portions of other metals, for silver the most common being copper. The amount of silver in the alloy sets the standard. What we call sterling silver in the United States and what the British call silver plate or plate consists of 925 of 1000 parts pure silver.

Elsewhere in Europe, the propor-

Previous pages, left: *A collection of early 17th-century pomanders. The largest is German and has sections for various spices and herbs, identified inside the gilt lid.* Right: *English counter and token boxes made from 1660 to 1730. Historic moments were engraved on each silver or paper counter, making them portable lessons.*
Clockwise from upper left: *An 18th-century Neoclassic teapot with an engraved coat of arms. Handles, usually ebony or blackened boxwood, were cool to the touch when the pot was filled with hot tea.*
Two double and four single silver saltcellars, made about 1870.
Early silver utensils, including an ancient Roman spoon, a simple English ribbed spoon, an engraved folding spoon, and a French 17th-century fork.
What can be more elegant than a silver candelabrum used in the most classic way in the center of the table?

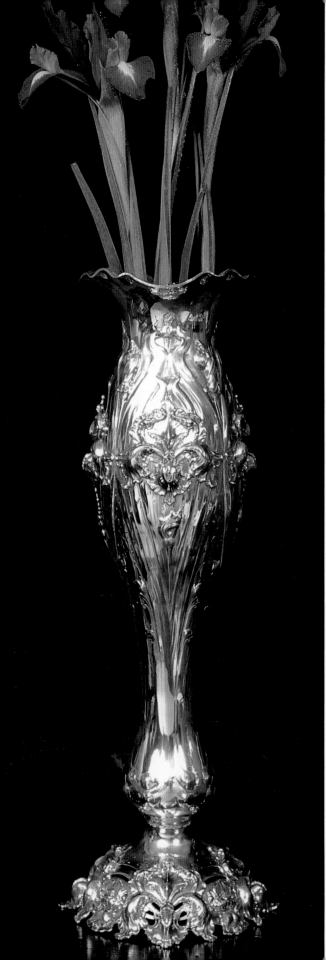

tions of silver to its alloy may be somewhat different. Very often on Continental pieces you will see 800 or 900, meaning that there are 800 or 900 parts of pure silver in the piece. Old French silver is often as high as 950 parts pure silver.

As anyone who loves old silver knows, individual pieces can look very different in color from one another, even though both may have the same amount of pure silver in them. This surface color and quality is known as the "bloom" or patina of the piece, something you should be aware of, especially when you are polishing silver. Clean the piece but take care not to overrub it.

I have always loved the elegance of old English silver. In Britain the silver trade has been carefully regulated since the end of the twelfth century. Since the thirteenth century, the Worshipful Company of Goldsmiths was entrusted with the task of hallmarking. It still is. Before silver could be sold, it had to be assayed in the Goldsmith's Hall, usually in an unfinished state. There it was given the hallmarks, small letters and symbols impressed into the surface, usually on the bottom.

Previous pages: *A drawing room influenced by the sophisticated taste of the 18th century. The rich walls are festooned with garlands of nuts and pinecones, and a tea table is set for tea. A Georgian silver teakettle on a stand (right) is kept warm by the spirit lamp beneath it.*
Left: *A sterling silver vase, made about 1910 by G. W. Shiebler and Co. of Brooklyn, with irises intricately worked into the base and sides.*
Right: *An intriguing corner of A La Vieille Russie in New York City—the cigarette case and frame are by Fabergé, the unusual silver breadbasket is lined with a trompe l'oeil napkin, and the nephrite box closes with a jeweled clasp. All were made in Moscow in the late 19th century at the pinnacle of Russian craftsmanship. They are just some of the treasures to be found in this wonderful place.*

English silver is still assayed and hall-marked. On old English silver there will often be a series of these marks, which tell you something about the piece. The following marks will be found on a piece of English silver, sometimes in combination with other marks:

• The *standard mark* or symbol of the lion passant, the form of a lion walking to the left, indicates sterling quality. It was introduced in 1544 and guarantees the 92.5 percent sterling standard.

• The *date letter* or assay mark shows us the year the silver was assayed and enables us to determine the date it was made. A different letter of the alphabet was used for each year. This letter was surrounded by a shield or other shaped outline. Both it and the typeface of the letter changed each year also.

• The *mark of origin* denotes where a piece was made. For example, a leopard's head represents London, an anchor Birmingham, and a crown Sheffield.

• Because few people could read, the earliest *maker's marks* were also symbols. By the seventeenth century this had changed, and letters, usually the maker's initials, appeared instead. For example, the famed English silversmith Paul de Lamerie registered his mark as LA in 1712, when the first two letters of the family name were required to be used. He changed it in 1733 to PL.

• The *duty mark,* used from 1784 to

Above left: *A George II tureen by Thomas Gilpin and pieces of Coalport china sit center stage in James Robinson, a New York City store that is always worth a visit if you love or collect old silver. Fifty-seventh Street is still home to a group of wonderful antiques shops, including S. J. Shrubsole, another place for fine silver.*
Left: *Elsewhere in the store, an impressive selection of heavy silver trays hang on special hooks. The rims are decorated with various kinds of ornamentation, including gadrooning.*

1890, depicts the reigning monarch's head and indicates that the duty or luxury tax on the piece had been paid. This started during the reign of George III and ended late in the reign of Queen Victoria.

Obviously, you will never be able to remember all these marks. There is a wonderful book to help you decode them entitled *Bradbury's Book of Hallmarks,* compiled by Frederick Bradbury. You can buy this little book in bookstores and often in shops that carry old silver. It gives all the marks for British and Irish silver and for Old Sheffield plate. It fits right into your pocket and is very handy to have with you. When you're tucking this away, also put in a small magnifying glass. I find it essential to have one for examining old silver. Some of the marks are minuscule or timeworn, and details may be difficult to see with the naked eye.

Two other very informative books for your silver library are *English Goldsmiths and Their Marks* and *The Illustrated History of English Plate,* both by Charles J. Jackson. Finally, there is *Old English Plate* by Wilfred Joseph Cripps, published in 1881, which I found at a library sale in the country. House and yard sales are often good places to find old or out-of-print books for your reference library.

Though English silver was highly regarded, it was not long after the settlers came to America before there were quality makers of very fine pieces on this side of the Atlantic as well. Although Paul Revere is the best known early American silversmith, there were others as well, in Boston, New York City, and Philadelphia, the silver-making centers of the New World. The forms of American silver largely mirrored English examples, but their design and execution were usually simpler.

Like English silver, American silver was also marked, although in different ways. In many cases, the maker or craftsperson put his mark on a piece, but by the mid-nineteenth century, because of the shift from craft to industry, the mark was

sometimes the manufacturer or retailer's. We sometimes find the words "dollar," "pure coin," or initials "C" or "D" stamped into pieces made after 1830. After 1860, "sterling" generally appears on appropriate pieces. It is important to be able to decipher these marks. A good reference book is essential, and *American Silversmiths and Their Marks* by Stephen G. Ensko is one of the best.

Although English and American silver may be a collector's primary focus, there are wonderful examples of the silversmith's craft from other countries as well—France, Italy, Germany, Austria, Russia, Scandinavia, Belgium, and The Netherlands—and all have their own silver-making traditions and marks. I have an elegant silver evening purse that once belonged to my grandmother, brought back from a long-ago trip to France. It is lined with soft, dove-gray leather and still has its tiny ivory-capped powder puff. When my mother was a little girl, it was given to her to hold so that she would be quiet while her picture was taken. This sepia-toned photograph of my mother now sits on a table in our living room. And the little reticule now belongs to one of my nieces.

The decoration of silver takes many forms. The following techniques are those you will most often come across. They were used alone and in combination, on solid silver as well as plated silver and other metals.

• *Engraving* is the cutting of lines and patterns into the surface of a piece. Any inscription—from that on a loving cup to that on a golfing trophy—is usually engraved. Coats of arms and initials are done this way too. "Bright cut" is a kind of engraving in which a special tool was used to pick out tiny bits of silver while at the same time burnishing the surface.

• *Chasing* is any ornamentation on a piece of silver achieved with a hammer and punch, working from the front or outside.

It results in raised and depressed areas and gives dimension to a piece. Flat chasing produces decoration in very low relief.

• *Repoussé* and *embossing* are interchangeable terms. The technique is similar to chasing, but the work is carried out from the back or inside of a piece, resulting in even greater depth. Embossing and chasing are often found in combination. Goblets, tea urns, tureens, and other objects that have scrolls, flowers, shells, and other domed designs are usually combinations of these two techniques. A frequent application of repoussé was *gadrooning*— a decorative raised border around a piece such as a candlestick or the rim of a porringer. The opposite of gadrooning is *fluting*, which is grooved in, instead of out.

• *Piercing* is simply making perforations in the silver. For example, pierced saltcellars are fairly common. They are often lined with blue glass dishes.

• *Gilding* is the fusion of gold onto the surface of a piece. Objects were gilded on the outside for ornamental purposes and to get the most from a small quantity of the precious metal. Egg cups and saltcellars were often gilt on the inside to protect the silver from corrosive damage.

Decorations such as these were done not only on sterling silver but on old Sheffield plate and electroplate as well. The term plate can be confusing to Americans. The English use it to mean both solid or sterling silver and articles of silver in general. A family's "plate" is its collection of silver, handed down from generation to generation. We Americans use the term

Above left: *Dramatic use of candles creates a special mood. Here, Russian, English, and American brass candlesticks are especially effective en masse.*
Above: *Examples of the simplicity and grace of pewter forms. American pewter design generally followed the silver styles of England.*

plate when we talk about something that is electroplated.

Old Sheffield plate and electroplate were the two primary substitutes for silver. The process for making Sheffield plate was discovered in 1742 by Thomas Boulsover. It was made in England from then until approximately 1850. It is simply thick plates of silver fused under very high temperature to both sides of a copper ingot, flattened into sheets, then rolled out, and fashioned into candlesticks, tea caddies, teapots, and myriad other forms. Making it was labor-intensive; however, the cost was so much less than solid silver that Sheffield plate became very popular for domestic use. The styles and designs followed those of solid silver, and old Sheffield plate is very sought after and highly prized today. The marks for old Sheffield plate are also in *Bradbury's Book of Hallmarks*.

A similar plating process was invented in Germany, but the silver was fused to nickel instead of copper. This is called German silver and you will occasionally come across examples of it.

Around 1840, the electroplate process was developed in England. Quite simply, an object made of white metal was dipped in a bath of silver. Electroplate replaced old Sheffield plate almost overnight. American craftspeople were also quick to adopt this new method. Reed & Barton in Massachusetts and the Rogers Bros. in Connecticut were the largest

Far left: *A 19th-century American painted cast-iron bunny doorstop holds a country gate open.*
Left: *Painted tin watering cans on the front steps—the top one is hand painted and the beige one, stenciled.*
Below: *This may appear to be a collection of flower baskets, but in fact it is a group of painted cast-iron doorstops made in America in the late 19th century. Cast iron, with its weight and durability, was frequently used for such practical objects but often given a touch of whimsy as well.*

makers of fine plated silver in America.

Many other metals have been used over the centuries to fashion beautiful, decorative objects. Among them are

• *Brass,* an alloy of copper and zinc. It has been used to make many objects, such as kettles and trivets. Many American settlers, for whom silver was too costly, brought treasured brass candlesticks with them.

• *Bronze,* an alloy of copper and tin and one of the best casting metals. It has been made into ritual food vessels in China, gilt decorative ornaments known as ormolu, and all manner of cast sculpture, such as the wonderful horses of San Marco in Venice. The patina on old bronze is very important to its beauty. Caused by oxidation, it may be green, blue, brown, or black.

• *Copper,* a naturally occurring reddish-colored metal. Because of its excellent heat-conducting qualities, it was used for many kitchen utensils that are now highly prized. Old pots and their covers,

molds, spoons, sieves, and other items all look wonderful adorning a kitchen wall.

• *Iron,* a natural metal of great strength that is known primarily for its industrial applications and has also lent itself to ornamental uses such as cast-iron doorstops, cooking pots, and fireplace andirons, as well as garden benches and other outdoor pieces.

• *Lead,* a soft metal derived from lead ore. It weathers well outdoors, resisting corrosion, and was used in a decorative way for architectural ornament, fountains, and garden sculpture.

• *Pewter,* an alloy of primarily tin, copper, and antimony. Because pewter is a relatively soft metal, it became the practice to remelt and recast old pieces when they began to show signs of wear. For this reason, old pewter from the seventeenth and eighteenth centuries is rare today. The beauty of the finest pewter lies in its clean lines, its color, and the quality of its construction.

Like silver marks, pewter marks can

be confusing. If you collect pewter, you should have a reference book of marks. Ledlie Irwin Laughlin's *Pewter in America,* for American makers, and Howard Herschel Cotterell's *Old Pewter: Its Makers and Marks* for English, Scottish, and Irish pewter are two good ones.

• *Tin,* produced from tin ore and used to plate very thin sheets of iron from which pieces of tinware are made. Because tin does not tarnish and resists organic acids, it was considered ideal for the kitchen. In flea markets and antiques markets, you often come across old tin biscuit boxes, tea caddies, serving trays, cookie cutters, and other pieces of kitchenware. While silver and pewter have a formal dignity to them, there is a cozy hominess to tinware that makes it very appealing.

The most prized decorative tinware is painted and is called japanned ware, toleware, or Pontypool after the town in Wales that became the center of British tinware. In general *japanned ware* refers to lightly decorated, hand-painted or stenciled tinware, while toleware, called "tole peinte" in France, refers to more formal, elaborately decorated pieces on which scenes, landscapes, or still lifes of flowers or fruit were painted.

Objects made of all these metals can add to the character of a room. Silver, though, is still the most cherished. It is synonymous with quality and the gentler aspects of life. We speak of silver-tongued eloquence and admire a singer's silvery tones. We search for silver linings and recognize the good fortune of those "born with a silver spoon in their mouths." Whether by birth or by choice, our lives can be touched with silver. Our homes are enhanced by graceful old pieces handed down over the years.

Below: *Early 19th-century coin silver spoons were hand-hammered instead of being cast, hence will have a light feel and usually bend easily.*
Overleaf: *Sugar tongs and serving pieces hang like laundry at an outdoor market.*

Caring for Silver & Other Metals

Silver should positively gleam. On the dinner table it should capture every flicker of candlelight. All metals need to be cleaned and cared for regularly. Here are some tips for looking after your prized silver pieces and antique metal objects.

- Silver should not be overpolished. Use elbow grease, but do not rub unnecessarily. When you must polish a piece, use a nonabrasive foaming paste cleaner, applied with a sponge. (I use Goddard's because my mother did, but there are lots of other fine foaming pastes available.) Use a cotton swab for hard-to-get-at areas. These cleaners are light and wash off easily. I always feel the conservative approach is the best, so I would avoid the silver dip method.

- Rinse off the foaming paste polish and use a soft natural-fiber cloth—well-washed terry cloth or linen, for example—or a paper towel to quickly dry the piece and bring up its shine. Pieces that have just a touch of tarnish discoloring their surface can be washed in warm soapy water instead of polished. Wash one piece at a time and dry each one immediately.

- When washing silver tea and coffeepots with wooden handles, be very careful because water and wood are natural enemies. Wax the wood with a good beeswax to seal it before you wash. Try not to immerse the wood in the water at all. If handles become loosened, have them repaired by an expert. Extra care should be taken with knives since the handles and blades are usually glued. Hand washing is a must.

- Be very careful when washing pieces such as candlesticks that have baize or felt on the bottom. Don't immerse in water. Instead, hold upside down and let the water run over 95 percent of the piece.

- Sulfur in the atmosphere is one of the chief causes of tarnish on silver. There are many ways to store silver, all based on keeping pieces out of the air. Many people use special silver bags with zippers or lined silver chests, which is fine. But the method I like best is putting each piece in its own plastic bag. This way you can look into your storage area and immediately see what's there.

- Use heavy-gauge self-closing plastic bags, the kind with the zipperlike closure. Make sure a piece is completely dry if you have just washed it before putting it in the bag since moisture also causes tarnishing. Press out as much air as you can before closing. Never use a rubber band to secure plastic bags around a piece of silver. They have sulfur in them, and this will penetrate the wrapping material.

- Dust your silver pieces no more than necessary. Dust has grit in it, and so dusting can scratch the surface of any metal, destroying its lovely patina as you work on it. Such patina results from proper use, not abuse, such as careless cleaning.

- When dusting, gently work from top to bottom of the piece. Make sure that the dust is off completely, not just rearranged on its surface. Use a very soft brush such as a watercolor brush. It should not be used on other objects. You should have a separate brush for each group of antiques that you dust to prevent transferring residue from one object to another. All of these brushes should be kept clean by washing them often.

- Never polish or wash bronze. The patina on a bronze object might easily be damaged or lost forever by overzealous cleaning or rubbing. Brass, copper, and pewter should be cleaned gently with good specific cleaners made just for that metal. Each piece may be dusted as needed, washed in warm water with mild soap, and dried immediately. All repair and restoration should be done by experts.

CHAPTER IV
TEXTILES

Antique textiles are among my great enthusiasms. My grandmother sewed superbly and made most of my clothes as I was growing up. I loved to pick out the fabrics for them. I think because of this I eventually went into the fashion business.

I enjoyed everything about my work, especially the quarterly trips to Europe for the collections. I delighted in the opportunity to travel to cities with beautiful museums, unusual restaurants, places to explore, and spectacular antiques shops and markets filled with more treasures than I had ever hoped to see.

The old fabrics were particularly wondrous—rich silk damask and velvet curtains with hand-knotted multicolored braid; finely embroidered Chinese cushions in once-brilliant colors; early continental samplers, long and thin; delicately wrought lace trimming sheer batiste pillow shams, often with ornate crowns and initials finely embroidered on them. The things one found then!

There were comparatively few people collecting antique textiles in those days, and I was often given a bit of old lace or fabric as a bonus by a dealer just because I was a kindred spirit. Times have changed quite a bit, but one thing is constant—textiles really do make all the difference in the way a room looks and feels.

John Fowler, one of England's most influential twentieth-century interior designers, was once asked to give his views on decorating. Fifty years later, his answers still ring true, and one of them is especially pertinent here—"Decoration is a logical compromise between comfort and appearance. A room must be essentially comfortable not only to the body but to the eye." Textiles do this in a very wonderful way. Their patterns, colors, textures, and "hand" not only create a beautiful environment, but also an intimate atmosphere that makes us feel relaxed. Deep-pile carpets, plump cushions, and luxuriously swathed windows—all help to insulate us from the sounds and abrasiveness of our increasingly hectic world.

Today there is a new awareness of the importance of antique textiles. In addition to their great decorative potential, they are fragments of the past that, perhaps more than any other antique, reflect the spirit and imagination of the people who made them. They are examples of skill, labor, and time extravagantly spent in creating objects of beauty that will never be duplicated.

One of my favorite types of textile is the shawl—especially Kashmirs and paisleys. The oldest shawls were made in Kashmir, India, arriving in Europe during the late-eighteenth century. Using the softest wool, from Himalayan mountain goats, weavers often took almost two years to finish a single shawl. The British in India began to bring back shawls to their loved ones, and the demand for these rare and beautiful shawls grew.

It took the Napoleonic wars to introduce the French to the Kashmir shawl. The Empress Josephine soon amassed a large collection of them and had all of France emulating her taste. Today, early Kashmir shawls are extremely rare, found mostly in museums, in collections started years ago, and, occasionally, at auction.

Not surprisingly, European weavers imitated the patterns of Kashmir shawls. The dominant motif was the familiar pine-

Previous page: *A 19th-century loveseat covered in needlepoint and petit point. Flowers and foliage entwine Chinese figures. Luxurious pillows are from the same period.*
Above left: *A beadwork angel on a Victorian velvet and needlepoint pillow edged with old soutache trimming.*
Right: *Several shawls, including one of wool tartan, are draped over a favorite easy chair and a table in this collector's corner.*

cone-shaped pattern, or "boteh" (spelled different ways), which we know today as paisley. This is because one of the centers of shawl-making was the town of Paisley, Scotland.

While Kashmir shawls were completely handwoven and embroidered, those from Paisley, Edinburgh, Norwich, Lyons, and other European textile centers were woven on draw-looms and, later, Jacquard looms. If you look at the back of a Kashmir shawl, you will see all the little details of hand embroidery scattered over the surface. The back of a paisley shawl, in most cases, will be very regular.

When I first started collecting shawls, there was very little written on the subject. My old standby was *The Paisley Shawl* by Matthew Blair, published in 1904. It still can be found at antiquarian booksellers. Happily, there are now some excellent new books, and I recommend *The Kashmir Shawl* by Frank Ames.

Shawls were extremely popular from about 1820 to 1870, when the crinoline gave way to the bustle and they became unfashionable. By then, most shawls were made for the masses, printed instead of woven and poorly manufactured. They all but disappeared, resurfacing recently to be collected and used in decorating.

 Shawls, used in many ways, add warmth and richness to a room.
Clockwise from upper left: *Paisley and Kashmir shawls from the mid-19th century stacked on a chest in Paul Jones, a shop on London's Kings Road that specializes in wonderful antique textiles.*
Two different striped paisley shawls that showed signs of wear have been made into pillows and used to cover the seat of a 17th-century Jacobean settle. The room is scented by clove-studded pomanders.
A desk set in a niche at the top of a staircase is covered with a paisley shawl and favorite old desk accessories.
A long Kashmir shawl is the perfect shape for this 19th-century daybed. A Biedermeier box and table are at its foot.

They are perfect for throwing over the back of a chaise or arm of a chair, to snuggle up under. They can be used to cover a round table where small collections are grouped. They are also terrific for hiding the fact that an old, well-loved sofa is showing some wear. I have a friend who gives her living room a fresh look by covering two such sofas in crisp, white Marseilles bedspreads in summer and rich, warm paisley shawls in winter.

If a shawl is damaged or worn out, and is not particularly rare, it can be made into pillows or pieced and used on a bed. There are as many ways to decorate with shawls as there once were to wear them.

Like the shawl, lace added elegance and prestige to a woman's wardrobe. Its exquisite beauty was a luxury because of the time and skill it took to make it, and its cost sometimes rivaled that of jewelry. Jane Austen, when given a lace-trimmed cloak by her sister in 1800, wrote thanking her, "My cloak came on Tuesday, and tho' I expected a good deal, the beauty of the lace astonished me. It is too handsome to be worn, almost too handsome to be looked at." Haven't you sometimes felt that way too, when you looked at something too beautiful for words?

Lace has long been admired and respected. It is made of linen thread, or, sometimes, silk, gold, or silver. There are two main types: needle lace and bobbin, or pillow, lace. Needle lace, the older, is a type of self-supporting embroidery made with a single needle and thread, using the buttonhole stitch. Bobbin lace requires bobbins, usually of bone, wood, or metal. It is made by sticking pins into a muslin-covered pillow through a paper pattern and winding the weighted bobbins of thread around the pins. Sometimes hundreds of bobbins are used at once. Both these laces are made by hand, and there are an enormous number of designs. There is also machine lace, which is less desirable but some of which was very well made.

Collecting lace can be fascinating, but

Previous pages, left: *These fine lace and batiste pillow shams, from about 1880, once belonged to a Belgian noble-woman whose coronet and monogram are embroidered on each one. The screen in the background is French.* Right: *Edwardian embroidered tulle boudoir pillows nestled in one corner of a small sofa in Gerry Tandy Antiques, Peekskill, New York. The hand-painted canvas window shade behind the sofa was done about 1920.*

Above: *An old, creamy damask tablecloth is always a rare find. This oversized rectangular one covers a round table and falls in opulent folds to the floor.*

Right: *An inviting chair and footstool make this bathroom look especially sophisticated. The towel rack holds interesting bits and pieces of a Victorian linen collection, and a china dish keeps lace-trimmed guest towels at hand.*

it also can be frustrating. Lace is a very complex subject, spanning centuries and continents, and if you collect you should be able to identify and recognize the different varieties of technique used in the various lace-making centers. Three very good books that will help you are *The History of Lace* by Mrs. Bury Palliser, an old classic written in 1910, *The Identification of Lace* by Pat Earnshaw, a current paperback book, and *An Illustrated Guide to Lace* by Emily Reighe, which includes pictures of the different laces.

Collars, cuffs, lappets, fans, veils, and trimmings were often made of lace. Wealthy or well-placed people had collections of lace, some passed down from generation to generation. It could be easily removed, laundered, and attached to another garment. If you are fortunate in finding an early piece of lace such as this, consider having it mounted on acid-free paper and framed. It will be protected and you can still enjoy it.

Lace-trimmed pieces from the nineteenth century are less rare and, if properly taken care of, can be used in the home. Hankies can be framed or made into small pillows. Nothing is prettier than freshly ironed linen and frothy lace pillow shams and bedcovers. In the dining room, creamy old damask cloths and napkins add a great feeling of luxury. Heavy lace-trimmed linen guest towels are a thoughtful amenity in guest rooms and baths.

Just as women made most laces, they also were responsible for creating the quilts that we have come to treasure. In America especially, quilt-making was a strong tradition. Many American girls filled their hope chests with thirteen quilts, the last being the bridal quilt. These were made with the help and love of family and friends and had great significance in a young woman's life. They were one of the few possessions listed in women's wills to be passed on to another generation. The esteem in which they were held is one reason they have survived.

I love old quilts and prefer to use them folded at the end of a bed in order to extend their lives. However, if the quilt is well worn but still useable, it can be re-backed and function, if not as a bedcover, then on a window or as a table cover.

The quilts I think most interesting are those that were made from printed cottons, sometimes remnants of women's dress fabric. The earliest printed designs were inspired by Indian fabrics. In fact, the words *chintz* and *calico* are of Indian origin. *Chintz* is a variation of *chints*, meaning "colored," and *calico* derived from Calcutta, a cloth-making center. The renowned Oberkampf firm in France was the center of toile-making. The word *toile* simply means "cloth," but came to be used for Oberkampf's printed cottons and linens, or toiles de Jouy, which were one-color designs on a plain, usually beige or off-white background. Many of these printed pictures commemorate history just the way decoration on pottery does. From woodblock to copperplate to roller, by the mid-nineteenth century printed fabrics were widely available.

The pieces and fragments of printed cottons that have survived are treasured by collectors. Because they are very delicate, they should be treated gently. A group framed on a wall is far less likely to be damaged than a pillow on a sofa, which people will be leaning against and handling.

Above left: *These late 19th-century lace curtains, found in Paris in the Marché aux Puces, create a special feeling in this room. Under the bay window, an English footstool from about 1750 holds a generous bowl, now filled with potpourri, that has been in the family for years.*
Left: *Worn quilts have been relined and hung on either side of a net lace curtain. Another quilt covers the bed.*
Right: *Pale-colored shells, including a framed sailor's valentine, perfectly complement the 1930s Madeira-embroidered cloth on the table. The china jugs are from Putnam's in London.*

Rare pieces should be kept rolled or flat in acid-free tissue and boxes.

There is now an awareness of how fragile all old textiles are and how carefully they must be preserved. Cloth begins to deteriorate almost from the moment it is made—when first subjected to sunlight, air, and pollution. There is a great temptation to try home remedies to clean a piece of fabric. Washing, dipping, ironing, spraying, or using any of the many potions available can cause irreversible damage. Old dyes will usually run.

If you have found a rare piece or have something that has been in the family for generations, I urge you to take it to a fabric restorer, museum curator, or historical society for advice before you do anything to it. Though the antique textiles you buy should be in pristine condition, this isn't always possible. The renewed interest in old textiles has given rise to many restoration services. Some of the best are listed in Chapter Eight.

The one family of antique textiles that has always been valued is that of carpets and tapestries. Over the centuries, many people have come under their spell. I was talking recently about antique carpets with Doris Leslie Blau, whose New York shop overflows with exquisite rugs from all over the world. She said, "I have always loved carpets. The carpet is an art form that brings all the tactile senses to life from the moment you come into a room. The designs and colors create such movement. Your eye travels from the floor up, not the wall down. An old rug has tremendous personality, which you can feel setting the tone right away."

There are so many kinds of carpets —from all the various orientals to French Aubussons to English Axminster and Wilton to American Navaho, hooked, and rag rugs. The range is vast, their history fascinating. Carpets were not always used on the floor. Until the eighteenth century floors were left bare and carpets covered things like tables and coffers and were brought out when needed.

Buying a good antique carpet is probably one of the greatest investments you will make in your home—not just in terms of money, but of having something that you will live with and look at every day. Examining and buying rugs requires research. A good place to start is with one of the many current books on the subject. Carpets have been well researched. Having a good dealer will be an important asset as well. Valuable rugs have been imitated widely and often only a trained eye can separate the wheat from the chaff.

Tapestries have been woven since the Middle Ages. Made of wool, they covered the uneven, cold stone castle walls and added warmth and beauty to an otherwise dark setting. They were portable, quickly rehung as the nobility traveled from one castle to another, and even accompanied their owners into battle. In France one Burgundian noble had so many that he built a special vault to hold them, and in England Henry VIII possessed two thousand at one time. With kings as custodians and nobility as customers, it is no wonder that tapestries were considered symbols of wealth and power.

Most of the French tapestries that

Previous page: *A fragment of French toile de Jouy, about 1785. It depicts a Crowning of Roses, a popular annual ceremony in 18th-century Europe. This piece is from Elinor Merrell's shop in New York City, where there are always extraordinary textiles to be found.*
Clockwise from upper left: *Woven into a 19th-century English rag rug, a black cat seems to cavort with a carpet ball. The smaller rug sits atop a larger, patterned one. The English country washstand has a hand-painted top.*
A white cat is worked into a needlepoint doorstop. The rug beneath it is also needlepoint from later in the century.
Kilim carpets in unexpected places, hung as curtains and made into pillows. They are enhanced by the deep colors of the tin tea canisters and pottery bowls.

have come down to us were made in workshops such as Beauvais, Aubusson, and Gobelin during the seventeenth and eighteenth centuries. Many of the most beautiful examples of verdure tapestries were made in Brussels in the sixteenth and seventeenth centuries. These botanical extravaganzas are filled with the rich shapes and colors of carefully observed growing things: flowers, fruits, plants, and trees. Today tapestries still look right. Their scale makes them particularly dramatic in spacious rooms with high ceilings.

In *Home Before Dark*, Susan Cheever's memoir about her father, John Cheever, there is an evocative description of just such a room in the home of a friend: "The center of the house was a three-story living room, which had huge leaded windows facing north and south and dark wood paneling up to about ten feet. The room was painted dark red; on one wall hung a tapestry of Barabbas returning to Cyprus, and on the other walls were Dutch and Italian old master portraits in heavy gold frames. The furniture was antique but comfortable and shabby, and the sofas and chairs bore unmistakable signs of the family dogs' license to sleep wherever they pleased. You could sink into one of those sofas and look upward into the rich shadows under the roof, . . . or let your eye rest on a painting, or just drift, and centuries of quiet seemed to sift down through the cathedral light."

While the weavers of carpets and tapestries were mostly men, women have been solely responsible for the vast majority of needlework that has so motivated collectors in recent years. Working quietly in their parlors, they produced marvels

Above left and left: *French Aubusson carpets with their graceful, swirling beauty, beneath needlepoint footstools and an ottoman from the 19th century. Aubusson carpets have a flat weave, typical of that on wall tapestries. Their designs reflected the architectural motifs of the rooms they were made to fill.*

out of cloth, needle, and thread. Each kind of needlework has its own special charm and identity: samplers, silk work, stumpwork, crewelwork, white work, beadwork, and needlepoint to list a few.

Down through the ages, needlework is often the only record of women's achievements. In one of my favorite books on the subject, *Plain and Fancy*, Susan Burrows Swan writes, ". . . needlework, in addition to being the most important contribution made by early American women to the decorative arts, was also their most acceptable outlet for creative expression and, indeed, in many instances the only concrete evidence of their endeavors. Needlework tells us a good deal about what it was like to be a woman in early America."

You may be drawn to one category of needlework, such as samplers, or to subject matter, such as mourning pictures, or to that of a certain period, such as stumpwork. Your collection may have a definite

Previous pages: left page, clockwise from top left: *An 18th-century Beauvais tapestry filled with extravagant foliage and depicting the god Pan in a woodland glade creates a backdrop.*
An intricate pattern of Victorian beadwork on a small cushion.
A needlepoint pole screen, every bit as decorative as a painting.
A graceful angel, embroidered in beadwork, about 1880.
A needlepoint rug, about 1860, used as a bedcover. The other floral patterns on the bed-curtains, carpet, and painting continue the flowery motif.
A crewelwork screen defines a separate dressing area in a bedroom.
Right page, clockwise from top left: Wool needlework pieces from the 19th century, worked in different stitches, once probably destined to be bellpulls.
Needlework pillows give a relaxed and cozy look to a living room.
Plump Berlin work and beadwork pillows, piled high on a chintz sofa.
Queen's stitch covering the seat of an early 18th-century oak chair. Accessories on the table re-create an inviting fireside scene from the time.
A panel of French Beauvais tapestry with its muted colors in an English Regency giltwood cheval fire screen.
Left: *Today we are aware of how irreplaceable rare, old textiles have become. These delicate pieces must be properly conserved and restored. Leave them in the care of experts, like the one at left, instead of trying home remedies.*
Above left: *A rare and charming collection of French beadwork from the late 17th to early 18th centuries. Most of the very fine individual beads can only be seen with a magnifying glass.*
Above: *A group of 19th-century beadwork sewing accessories, including pincushions. The little handmade paper boxes at the bottom were used to sort and keep the beads. Each box is labeled according to color.*

focus or just be filled with things you love. However you shape it, any assortment of needlework is certain to please the eye and delight many times over.

These are some of the types of needlework that are most popular today:

• *Samplers* at first were simply records, a sampling of the many stitches, some quite complex, and techniques that could be used in embroidery. They were also a young girl's first introduction to needlework. Working with linen or silk threads on a linen background, she practiced her stitches so that one day she would be prepared to embroider her trousseau and sew the household linens that her own home would require.

Over time, samplers became much more than mere exercises. Though guided by instructors, a young girl could stretch her imagination and work wonderful thoughts, scenes, and animals into her samplers. Such pieces of fancy needlework are very personal, often tender reminders of the past. Many have been handed down through the generations in a family. They are highly prized by collectors, all the more valuable for being signed and dated, their provenance above reproach. Age, however, is not as important as condition and pictorial beauty in making a sampler, or other piece of needlework, valuable. Of the many books on needlework, an excellent one is *American Needlework Treasures*, by Betty Ring, one of America's most knowledgeable collectors of samplers.

• *Silk work* is embroidery with silk

 Old tassels and trimmings add richness to a room.

Left: *A collection of 18th- and 19th-century examples in linen, silk, and metallic threads.*

Above left: *Tassel tiebacks used to pull back bed hangings.*

Above: *A French opaline lamp sits on a table in front of paper taffeta curtains with oversized tassels.*

thread on a silk background. Using the skills learned in making samplers, women stitched elaborate scenes. They were inspired by paintings and engravings, or they designed their own pieces. Mourning pictures were frequently worked in silk.

• *Stumpwork* is a combination of techniques. Figures and animals were first worked on linen, then stuffed and appliquéd to an embroidered satin background so that they stood out in relief. Popular in the later seventeenth century, these three-dimensional creations have a cheerful, childlike quality. They were often framed like samplers or used to cover boxes, purses, and mirror frames.

• *Crewelwork* is embroidery with wool on a linen background. The word *crewel* actually refers to a twisted, worsted yarn, but we use it to mean this kind of work in general. Crewel embroidery was preferred for such large pieces as counterpanes and bed hangings, where large flowers and leaves seem to float on air. Small pieces such as seat covers, pockets, petticoat borders, and pictures were also done in crewel.

• *White work* is simply white embroidery on a white fabric background. In the early nineteenth century it was a favorite technique for embroidering christening gowns and baby clothes, as well as for very delicate bodices and handkerchiefs.

• *Beadwork* is needlework that incorporates small glass beads in some way in the design. In the eighteenth and nineteenth centuries, beads were embroidered onto a piece of canvas and made into slippers, ornate pictures, sewing and desk accessories, and reticules.

• *Needlepoint*, as we know it, is the working of stitches, usually in wool or silk, over the threads of a canvas. It includes everything from the simple tent stitch to the Berlin work of the Victorian era, in which intricate pictorial patterns were followed almost like paint-by-numbers. Needlepoint was used for upholstery, footstools, rugs, fireplace fans, pillows, wallets, and slippers. It is as popular today as it was when it was first made.

Trimmings are a textile accessory. Fringe, tassels, gimp, and braid can give definition to the furnishings in a room. Writing in 1872, Charles Locke Eastlake, in *Hints on Household Taste*, says, "While on the subject of curtains, it may be as well to add a few words regarding the employment of fringe. Fringe . . . was originally nothing more than the threads of silk or woollen stuff, knotted together at the ragged edge, to prevent it from unravelling further. By degrees they came to be knotted at regular intervals, so that at length this contrivance grew into a system of ornament, which survived the necessity of its original adoption. But long after the use of detached fringe, it continued to be made of threads alone, and threads of the same quality as the stuff." When a length of old fringe or braid is properly used, it can strike just the right note in a room.

Phillips, one of the oldest auction houses in London, has a textile auction almost every month. I remember the first time I went there, over fifteen years ago—I couldn't believe my eyes. There were rare laces, eighteenth-century English Spitalfields silks, dazzling Chinese robes, William Morris draperies, and paisley shawls everywhere. For the first time, I could touch a piece of early stumpwork and look at every stitch. I held things in my hands that I'd only read about or seen behind glass in museums. It was like waking up from a wonderful dream and finding a trunk of treasure.

A corner of the textile department's storeroom at Phillips Blenheim Place Galleries in London before a big autumn auction. Costumes, samplers, laces, pillows, and old books on textiles are among the items about to be cataloged for the sale. This piece of 17th-century stumpwork, in a frame from a later date, has a biblical scene in the center, with exotic-looking animals, a lion, deer, unicorn, and leopard in the four corners. It is just one of the many treasures that await lucky bidders at auctions like this all over the world.

The auction rooms offer an unequaled opportunity to educate yourself in the decorative and fine arts. You can really examine things up close—not just old textiles, but all kinds of antiques. It is a good idea to go to the previews and ask questions. Put your name on the mailing list and take advantage of the lectures many auction houses offer. You will hear the experts discuss their fields.

Attending auctions in your area of interest will give you a feeling for what is happening in the marketplace. Even though the bidding is not always indicative of what an item is worth—reason sometimes goes out the window—you do get to see a broad spectrum of what is happening. The large auction houses like Christie's and Sotheby's have some thirty or more departments, and their catalogs can become irreplaceable reference books. When the collection of a respected collector is being auctioned, the catalog, especially its photographs, becomes a record. It offers a last look at a collection lovingly and painstakingly gathered over a lifetime, and a glimpse of the mind behind it.

Several years ago, I bought a silkwork picture at an auction of old and rare samplers. Though nothing more than a small bit of cloth covered with stitchery, this humble piece has a power undiminished by time, as do all fine, old handmade textiles. I have since been in touch with the descendants of the woman who skillfully embroidered it in 1774 and have learned a bit about her family. Such an experience confirms the joy of being a collector, a joy that awaits everyone who loves old things, especially old textiles, as I do.

Right: *A border of 18th-century silk embroidered in vivid colors.*
Far right: *A sampler made in Pennsylvania and signed Lydia Hoopes, 1774. The spray of flowers and vines is worked in a variety of stitches, including satin stitch.*
Overleaf: *Lengths of 18th-century English Spitalfields silk cover a dressing table and are held aloft by two dancing putti.*

Caring for Antique Textiles

Old textiles need loving care. The idea that these vulnerable, delicate pieces have survived for centuries is extraordinary. Over the years, someone cared enough to treat them properly. Now it's our turn.

◉ Each type of old textile should be cleaned in a different way, so it is always best to approach cleaning very cautiously and conservatively. Do no try to wash or dry-clean anything valuable without first consulting a textile expert. The damage done to fragile textiles can be irreversible.

◉ Most all white cottons and linens can be gently hand-washed in warm water with a neutral detergent. (This is available at museum supply companies listed in Chapter Six.) If you must use an alternative, use something gentle like Ivory Flakes. Never use chlorine bleach as a whitener because it weakens the fibers and hastens disintegration of the piece of fabric. Rinse with clear water several times. Do not wring the item out by twisting it. It could easily tear when wet. Lace or any delicate things should be put into a net bag before hand-washing to support them properly. If the lace is very old or valuable, do not wash it yourself.

◉ After washing, each item should be dried flat on a white cotton towel. Never hang a wet piece of cloth to dry. The weight of the water, combined with gravity, may rip it. Never dry anything in the sun, because sun is a bleaching agent, and the piece could fade.

◉ Never wash any colored textile—for example, a sampler, quilt, or paisley shawl. In most cases, the colors may not be permanent and may run, ruining the piece beyond repair. Consult with an expert before submitting these items to any cleaning treatment.

◉ As for needlepoint pillows and upholstered pieces, in most cases you can clean them sufficiently by carefully vacuuming up surface dust with a low-powered, hand-held vacuum cleaner. No carpet needs constant vacuuming. Using the small vacuum just on those sections that need attention will help prolong the life of the carpet. Large antique carpets should be professionally cleaned and stored. I would seek the advice of a reputable dealer. If they do not handle cleaning themselves, they can certainly recommend a trustworthy service to you.

◉ The worst enemy of textiles is light. Sunlight breaks down organic fibers and dyes, fading and weakening them irrevocably. You can do certain things to protect your old fabrics. If they are framed, try to use ultraviolet-proof Plexiglas. Draw drapes and shades when the room is not in use. Turn your rug once a year. Keep very precious textiles out of direct sunlight. When not in use or on display, textiles should be stored in a dark, well-ventilated place. Temperatures should be fairly constant and humidity should be around 55 percent. Never store old textiles in damp basements or dry attics.

◉ Antique textiles should always be stored flat, never on hangers. If at all possible, roll rather than fold them. Folding creates sharp creases and weakens that area of the textile. If a large piece, a quilt, for example, cannot be rolled, take pieces of acid-free tissue and stuff them inside the folds to prevent deep creasing. Once or twice a year, refold items that have been stored folded to prevent permanent creasing.

◉ Always use acid-free tissue, tubes, and storage boxes when putting textiles away. Never use colored tissue or plastic bags. If you run out of acid-free tissue, a clean white cotton or linen sheet can also be used for this purpose. Loosely roll each item, trying not to overcrowd.

◉ If a piece is damaged, you should consult a textile conservator immediately. The only safe kind of repair is one that is easily reversible and appropriate for the piece. A good rule of thumb is that it is always better to do too little than too much to antique textiles.

CHAPTER V
GLASS

Remember that rich, ruby-red glass goblet catching the sun in a dusty shop window in the movie *Summertime*? It starred Katharine Hepburn, my favorite actress then (and now), visiting the most romantic city in the world and falling in love with a suave, handsome Venetian who owned an antiques shop! I loved the movie and each time I see a piece of deep-red glass I think of Venice—for many reasons.

Venice was already the center of glassmaking in the Western world in the thirteenth century and was further brought to prominence by the perfection of *cristallo*, or clear crystal glass, in the early sixteenth century. For hundreds of years, marvels of lavishly decorated, richly colored glass and remarkable mirrors flowed from the city's Murano workshops to the rest of Europe. James Morris, in his evocative book *Venice*, describes the early Venetians as "the only people in Europe who knew how to make a mirror."

Glass is still being made there today, and while the modern glass is a far cry from the brilliance of centuries past, Murano is still worth visiting in order to see the beautiful old glass in the Museo Vetrario. The museum is in the Palazzo Giustiniani, one of the island's few surviving seventeenth-century palaces and itself worth seeing.

The secrets of making glass were scrupulously guarded, as were the glassblowers, who were forbidden to leave Venice. Eventually, however, some did escape, first settling in Bohemia. There they produced pieces that reflected their Venetian heritage and made the fine and various types of Bohemian glass famous. Charlotte Brontë, in *Jane Eyre*, describes

a richly decorated drawing room in which sparkling ruby-red Bohemian glass stands atop a Parian mantelpiece, and this is what most of us think of today when we think of Bohemian glass. Frequently it had overlay designs of vines or grapes, especially appropriate on decanters or ewers.

Then, in England, lead or flint glass was developed, and with its superior refractory qualities, colorless transparency, and brilliance, it was a perfect material for the making of cut glass. The quality of this glass, made from the late-seventeenth century to the mid-nineteenth century, in England and Ireland, is unexcelled—shallow cut, scalloped or sawtooth edged, the simple shapes, including such items as drinking glasses, saltcellars, jugs, candlesticks, compotes, and other forms, are, I think, among the most lustrous and graceful glass ever made.

In young America, people lived in an almost glassless world, restricting its use to windows and other practical necessities. Then, in 1739, Caspar Wistar, working in New Jersey, began to make flint glass in decorative forms. Soon after, Henry William Stiegel in Pennsylvania set out to make glass that rivaled the best

Previous pages: *Creamy English and Irish cut glass, sitting on a lacy silver tray, make a fine background for fresh, colorful fruits and berries.*
Above left: *An early 19th-century oversized English decanter etched with the name "Hollands," a kind of gin made in the Netherlands.*
Right: *A delicate glass tiered cup, made in Germany in the 19th century. The three pieces fit into one another, each now filled with flowers.*
Overleaf, left: *In the center of the table, a 19th-century American pressed-glass punch bowl sits underneath a glass chandelier and is surrounded by glass candlesticks. All this gives the room an airy look.* Right: *A collection of American pressed and flint glass pieces, including cup plates encircling a compote filled with glass grapes.*

from abroad and which had a profound influence on the quality of American glass.

Today, when most of us think of old American glass, pressed glass may be one of the first types to come to mind, especially examples from the Boston and Sandwich Glass Company of Massachusetts. The firm made all kinds of glass but is best remembered for its pressed-glass pieces —cups, plates, pitchers, compotes, sugars, and creamers—all made in hundreds of different patterns from the very simple to the elaborate. There are many excellent books on the subject by Ruth Webb Lee, who wrote extensively on American glass.

Glass itself is an intriguing subject. A substance that looks so delicate and graceful, yet can be so substantial and hard, is nothing short of magic. Put very simply, glass is essentially silica (obtained from sand) and alkali fused by heat. The formulas vary. By adding metal oxides, different colors and qualities of glass are obtained. There are three basic types, according to how it is made.

• *Free-blown glass* is the earliest kind. A lump of molten glass is attached to a hollow rod through which the glassmaker blows, while turning and shaping the piece. Various tools, including a pontil, are used to work the glass. Free-blown glass can sometimes be recognized by the pontil mark, or rough spot left by the pontil, usually on the bottom of the piece.

• *Blown molded glass* is made almost the same way, except that the glass is blown into a mold and removed. Blown three-mold glass was made in this way. This glass bears seam lines from the joins in the mold.

• *Pressed glass* is poured into the mold and then pressed with a weight. The technique, introduced in the nineteenth century, was the first significant innovation in glassmaking in thousands of years.

Reflective and transparent, glass can be left smooth and pristine, or it can be worked and embellished. There are many ways to decorate glass. Some are:

• *Cutting.* Cut glass is made by grinding the surface of the glass with a wheel and cutting sections away, leaving facets usually in a geometric pattern. For centuries, England has produced lead crystal ideal for cutting. America began to make outstanding pieces in the late-nineteenth century.

• *Engraving.* With a diamond point or copper wheel, cuts are made in the surface of the glass. Initials, words, or names of spirits, such as claret, are often engraved on decanters and other pieces. *Relief, stipple,* and *intaglio* are kinds of engraving.

• *Acid etching.* Achieved by using acid, this kind of decoration looks very much like frosting on glass.

• *Enameling.* Color is fused onto the surface of the glass to look as if it were painted on.

Glass truly brings a room to life. Small pieces grouped together, capturing and reflecting the light, animate a room as few things do. While browsing through my bookshelf the other day, I came across an old book on manners, *Millionaire Households,* written in 1903. In an early chapter entitled "When the Smart Set Dines," author Mary E. Carter captures the mood of long-ago dinners, writing, "After a while returning to the dining-room, we find it

Clockwise from upper left: *These early 18th-century English wineglasses, mostly engraved, with air-twist stems, are set on an unusual example of a fire screen that was used to protect one from the heat when sitting near the fireplace. Its glass back is engraved with a garland of oak leaves and acorns.*
Ormolu mounts support a 19th-century French cut-glass epergne with five separate vases, which is perfect for holding small flowers or ivy.
These cut-glass knife rests were originally made in full sets, like other glassware, one for each place setting. The saltcellar is Victorian silver and cut glass.

dazzling with polished silver and gold; at each place are exquisitely engraved crystal goblets for champagne, . . . and other drinking vessels, not less than five in a cluster, while in the midst of each sparkles one of ruby red or richest green. All these indicate the variety of choice wines to flow during the course of the banquet."

One of the joys of collecting glass is that it can really be used. As I mix patterns of china when creating a table setting, I also combine collections of drinking glasses. Different shapes in the same color or the same shapes in different colors can give a table unexpected personality.

On summer days, we often eat salads outside under our grape arbor. Using glass serving plates makes the meal look cool and even more inviting. A beautiful old glass punch bowl holds the greens, and unmatched clear glass pieces such as jam and relish dishes hold colorful salad makings. The glass mixes wonderfully with the colors and textures of fresh vegetables

Above, left and right: *Candelabra, especially those made of glass, add a note of luxuriousness and elegance to a room. They become quite dazzling when, complete with candles, they are reflected repeatedly in mirrors.*

Right: *An 18th-century French mirror provides a powerful focal point. Mirrors can be the most important accessories in a room, increasing and reflecting the light.*

Overleaf, clockwise from upper left: *A Nailsea glass collection displayed on a desktop—a small dish, a pair of knitting needles, and an assortment of pens. Nailsea glass can be recognized by its stripes of bright colors with white. It was made in England in the early 19th century.*

French latticinio glass, about 1840—the swirling patterns in this decanter and jug, and the surrounding vases and goblets, repeat the colors in the loveseat.

Pale delicate colors are a feature of St. Louis paperweights. This millefiori weight was made in France around 1850.

and fruits and country table linens.

Glass complements glass in wondrous ways. Glass paperweights on a glass table, for example, become an intricate collage of light and color. A glass candelabrum with cut-glass prisms, placed in front of a mirror, creates a double image of sparkle and elegance. Glass, I think, is one of the few things that really looks good when shown behind glass, in a bookcase or cabinet, perhaps.

How you decorate with and use glass can suggest new areas for collecting—for example, concentrating on glass of one color. There are some very beautiful examples of colored glass, especially from the mid-nineteenth century, when it became quite popular. All different colors were produced—from ruby or cranberry red, to cobalt or bristol blue, to vaseline or canary yellow, to mercury or silver, to milk glass.

Although transparency is one of the most familiar qualities of glass, opaque glass—known as satin or shaded glass—became popular in the 1880s. It has a dull finish and a velvety feel, and it usually has a white lining. Burmese, peachblow, mother-of-pearl, rainbow, and amberina are several of the different colors of satin or shaded glass.

Cameo glass is a colored glass in which the opaque outer layer of a light color is carved away from a darker background, looking almost like a cameo. The famous Portland vase, unearthed outside Rome in the sixteenth century and now

Above and right: *Two collections of silvered, or mercury, glass. Because it has a double thickness, with a silvery lining, this type of glass looks heavy but in fact is surprisingly light. It was made in the mid-19th century in America and England and was frequently fashioned into the ornamental forms seen here—tiebacks, vases, Christmas ornaments—by the mastery and skill of the glassblower.*

in the British Museum, is an example of cameo glass. Art Nouveau cameo glass made at the turn of the century by Gallé and Daum is much sought after now.

Also at the turn of the century, an unusual iridescent glass became very popular. Although it was made by glass factories such as Steuben, we associate it today with Louis Comfort Tiffany. He perfected the satiny-textured blown glass known as Favrile, which was sometimes called "peacock" iridescent. Art glass and Art Nouveau pieces are also often iridescent, in silvers, purples, blues, or golds.

Glass is a vast and varied subject. *A Short History of Glass* by Chloe Zerwick is a good starting point for any library on glass. This book is published by the Corning Museum in Corning, New York, where you can see one of the best collections of glass in the United States.

Even if you don't collect glass, there is one object for the home that I consider essential. A silvery mirror in a handsome

Color can be one of the most distinctive qualities of glass. In natural light, it is seen at its best. Glass can be arranged in little still lifes that create a kaleidoscope of color.

Previous page, left and right: *Two collections of 19th-century American colored glass pieces including cranberry, cobalt, and amethyst glass.*

Previous page, center: *Several early 19th-century American free-blown chestnut bottles, including one (third from the top) which is blown three mold.*

Above left: *A grouping of various forms of English green glass from James II in New York City dating from about 1835 to 1870.*

Left: *Bristol blue glass has extraordinary depth and often has gold decoration. These pieces date from 1780 for the footed glass bowl to 1840 for the decanter set and candlestick.*

Above: *Ruby-flashed or stained-glass vanity box, tumbler, and covered jar were made in the late 19th century.*

antique frame can be as enriching to a room as a painting. A very large mirror can almost seem to double the size of a room and all that's in it. It also increases the light and in a dark room can create an airiness that wasn't there before. For years I have collected old frames. Some are delicately carved and brightly gilded, some quite old and valuable, yet nobody seemed to want them. Since I am perpetually decorating, I thought I could always use them somewhere. With mirrors added, the frames have been given new life and now add a special quality to the rooms of my home.

Antique paperweights made of glass are intriguing too. Most were made in France, Germany, America, and England. Of these, the French paperweights—Baccarat, St. Louis, and Clichy—made from about 1840 to 1850 are truly exquisite. Among the most extraordinary and complex are the fine millefiori paperweights, meaning literally "a thousand flowers" and resembling for all the world a bouquet of massed flower heads captured in glass.

Paperweights are just one kind of glass object that can be collected—decanters, goblets, tumblers, bud vases, fruit baskets, epergnes, candlesticks, bells, inkwells, glass eggs and balls are just a few others. But when you are buying glass, more than with any other antique, you must know what you are doing. Glass has been reproduced and old forms imitated since the beginning. Most glass was not marked, so you must develop knowledge and an eye to be able to recognize the special qualities of fine old glass.

There are some little clues that can indicate age. For example, scratches on the bottom of a piece of old glass come from its being moved about, picked up and put down thousands of times. These signs of wear should be spread evenly and randomly, not all in one direction, over the bottom. Also there is a "feel" of old glass, a kind of oily softness or velvety patina,

that new glass simply doesn't have.

The presence of the pontil mark is not an infallible test of age. On many pieces of fine glass, such as paperweights, the glassmaker deliberately ground off the pontil mark as a fine finishing touch. Conversely, some modern glassmakers leave the pontil mark on their pieces. Nor can you depend on the ringing tone of a piece of glass as a test of age. Almost any good-quality glass will ring.

Glass that breaks cannot be easily repaired. A crack will always show. However, some damage can be obliterated by grinding and repolishing. For example, if the lip of a vase or bottle is chipped or cracked, it can be ground down. When examining glass, look at the proportions of the piece. If a decanter looks short in the neck, it may have been ground back. Also, be certain that the stopper is original to the decanter.

You can find wonderful antique glass pieces in America, Europe, and England —especially London. I was discussing antique glass with Lynne Stair, dealer and collector. She said, "It's hardly surprising that so much of the finest glass is to be found in London. After all, the very best cut glass was English and Irish. Perhaps this is all part of the British fondness for

Colorful glass on a table, coordinating with walls and china, always makes a dinner party setting much more striking. Charming, small bouquets of dried flowers and herbs, along with family portraits and Venetian mirrors, create the right background.

Previous pages, left: *An English Bristol blue decanter, about 1810, sits comfortably beside modern glassware from Venice.* Right: *American ruby glass and Depression glass in a regal red setting.* Left: *What better way to begin a day at an outdoor market than with a cup of hot tea? The giant blue-and-white willow teapot at Portobello Road in London beckons all who arrive on a chilly Saturday morning.*

port, Madeira, and sherry. They just expect there to be a beautiful cut-glass decanter on the sideboard."

Hunting for glass and other antiques in the outdoor markets of Europe is exhilarating. The markets are unlike anything in the United States in that they are open throughout the year, winter and summer. The Rome Flea Market, the Marché aux Puces in Paris, and London's many markets are among the sources for antiques discussed in Chapter Eight, which includes suggestions for exploring this world of collecting. Some people visit London just to go to the outdoor markets. There is such excitement, such anticipation—you really never know what you are going to find. Each week dealers come from all over England, bringing fascinating new merchandise with them.

As much fun as it is, it is also hard work. You will be getting up early, and the markets are not centrally located, so getting to them can be an unlooked-for adventure. They are very crowded and competition can be fierce. It can be dark and cold and rainy. But as much as I may complain, *nobody* can ever talk me out of going, ever. The hunt and the delight of discovery never lose their appeal.

Visiting the markets can also spark a new area of interest for you. I started collecting decanters because I kept seeing them in the London markets and they became irresistible. A collection of cut-glass decanters filled with colored liqueurs on a silver drinks tray is most welcoming. Finding and buying them also motivated me to study more about glass.

Years ago, when I lived in Florida, I

As many times as I've been there, the outdoor street markets of London are always a highlight of my trip. I invariably find something I can't live without. Here, in these markets, you can sometimes have the most fun.

Above: This is where you want to be on your first Friday in London—the entrance to the Bermondsey Market, also called the New Caledonian Market. Located across the Thames River, opposite the Tower of London, it can be difficult to find but is well worth the effort. The tables that fill the stalls are replenished each week by dealers who scour the countryside looking for new merchandise. Every table is laden with my favorite kinds of things, from English silver dressing table accessories and scent bottles to glass decanters and even chandeliers. Your chances of getting a bargain are good if you arrive nice and early.

Below: In Portobello Road, probably the best-known market, there are arcades, or mini-markets, where dealers exhibit their wares indoors. These make it worth going, even if the weather is poor, which is sometimes the case with year-round outdoor markets. If you have a choice, spring and fall are ideal times to shop for antiques in the London markets—or any of the British or European markets for that matter. There are usually fewer tourists, making the stalls less crowded and the prices more reasonable. The competition can be fierce as most dealers and shop owners cover these markets thoroughly when they are on buying trips in London. If you find something you want, don't hesitate, buy it then. There I am, doing just that, at six A.M. in Bermondsey.

started collecting bottles (a precursor to decanters, perhaps?). I found my first one —a bitters bottle—while exploring in the mangrove swamps in the Florida Keys. It was old, charming, and it cost nothing! I was hooked.

Today many people are collecting bottles with great enthusiasm—and now it costs something! I recently read that a rare deep-blue sarsaparilla bottle from 1850, found on a shelf in an old Connecticut farmhouse, was auctioned for thirteen thousand dollars. Age, rarity, shape, quality, and color—ranging from green, the commonest, to dark purple, the rarest—are the main criteria for bottle collectors. Some people collect only unusual shapes, such as figural bottles. Others look for early, hand-blown bottles, such as whiskey bottles, that are recognized by their pontil marks. The beautiful old labels of apothecary or medicine bottles can provide added interest.

And, of course, scent bottles can be especially beautiful. The delicacy of perfume bottles, and in fact of most glass, is one of its most enduring qualities. In the play *The Glass Menagerie,* by Tennessee Williams, Tom's memory of his sister Laura was stirred by different things. He says, "Perhaps it was a familiar bit of music. Perhaps it was only a piece of transparent glass. . . . I pass the lighted window of a shop where perfume is sold. The window is filled with pieces of colored glass, tiny transparent bottles in delicate colors, like bits of shattered rainbow."

Old bottles, found at the seashore, make very simple but elegant vases, massed atop an old American mantelpiece. Looking for, and finding, old bottles can become an engrossing pastime. Go to your local library or historical society. Search out the locations of old glassworks and refuse dumps in your town. A walk along coves and inlets at the water's edge can result in your finding a surprise treasure.

Caring for Glass Antiques

Glistening pieces of glass are closely related to ceramic works in that there is a vulnerability about them. Their delicate nature becomes all too apparent when these pieces are handled carelessly. The tips given here will help you to handle and care for your glass antiques.

- As with ceramics, never be in a rush when you are going to handle your glass objects. I find that simple chores, like washing a group of old wineglasses that belonged to my grandmother, can be quite satisfying if I am in the right mood. Because most glass is transparent and colorless, it can sometimes be hard to see, another reason for extra patience when working with glass.

- When picking up a piece of glass, always use both hands and always support the bottom of the piece. Never pick up more than one object at a time. If you're using a tray, make sure not to overload it.

- Fine, early, or valuable glass should be kept in closed shelves, cabinets, or something similar to protect it from too much dust or handling.

- Always hold a glass object gently in place when you dust it. Glass is light and the piece could tip over. Use a short, soft brush and slowly brush top to bottom.

- Never put old or fine glass in a dishwasher. When washing glass, use lukewarm water and a mild detergent. Make the same preparations that you would for washing ceramics—line the sink with towels or use a separate plastic bowl for washing.

- Wash only one object at a time. Never have more than one piece in the sink or basin at a time. The transparency of glass makes it difficult to see once it is in water.

- Do not soak glass for any length of time. Never put any glass that has been restored into water, since in many cases water-soluble glue may have been used to repair it.

- Be careful to rinse in very clean, clear water so as not to leave a slippery residue on the glass.

- When washing mirrors, use a wad of cotton instead of a cloth. This way you avoid touching the frame and possibly damaging it. I prefer not to reback the glass of my old mirrors. I love the charm of looking into a mirror that has seen hundreds of years of images.

- Air-drying is best for glass. Cover the table with paper towels before you set the wet glass down to dry. As with ceramics, this will prevent the piece from slipping or sliding off the table. If you must dry by hand, use a soft natural-fiber cloth or paper towel and wipe very gently, being sure not to catch the cloth or towel on any part of the glass. Pieces should be totally dry before being stored away.

- When storing glass, never put pieces so close together that they are vibrating against each other. Always leave some space between them, and be sure they are well back from the edge of a shelf. Try not to store them in wrapping, like tissue or newspaper, that may attract and hold dampness.

- Store the small objects in front of the large ones. Never put a small piece inside a large one.

- If you have a piece of glass, most likely a decanter or chandelier, that has developed a cloudy condition on its surface (sometimes this is referred to as "sick" glass), take it to a glass expert who can very often correct this problem. When storing decanters, remove the stoppers.

CHAPTER VI

PAPER

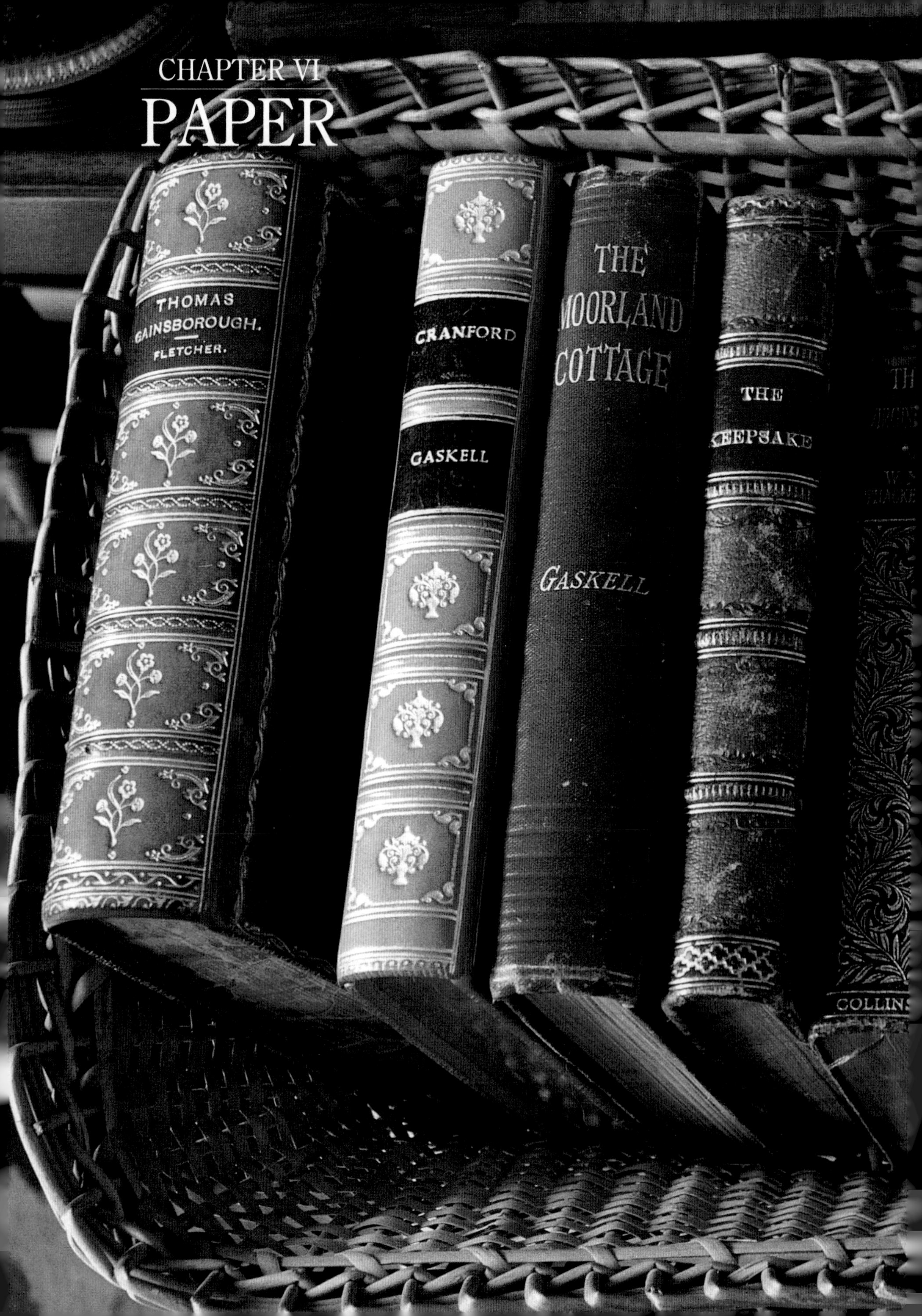

I love the inscriptions people write on flyleaves and the notes in margins; I like the comradely sense of turning pages someone else has turned, and reading passages someone long gone has called my attention to," writes Helene Hanff in *84 Charing Cross Road*, a very special book about loving books. Old books offer human companionship as do few other antiques. We enjoy them in so many ways—by discovering them, learning from them, and owning them.

There is a special feeling to the velvety leather bindings of old books. Edith Wharton and Ogden Codman wrote in 1897, in *The Decoration of Houses*, "Those who really care for books are seldom content to restrict them to the library, for nothing adds more to the charm of a drawing-room than a well-designed bookcase: an expanse of beautiful bindings is as decorative as a fine tapestry." I agree.

Even if you are fortunate enough to have a room that you call a library, I still think that books belong throughout the home. They give each room a human look that says someone lives here. Whatever room in my home I am in, I can always find a place to perch and a book to peruse.

My books have a tendency to accumulate. To keep things somewhat under control, and so I can find them easily, I like to arrange them by subject. Cookbooks and old books on housekeeping are on shelves in the kitchen. Gardening books are in a little sitting room, and in the bedroom Anthony Trollope's novels are shelved companionably with books by Angela Thirkell found over the years, mostly at yard sales. There are other ways of organizing, of course—by author or period, for instance—whatever is logical to you.

In "The Philosophy of Furniture," an essay Edgar Allan Poe wrote in 1840, he describes "some light and graceful hanging shelves, with golden edges and crimson silk cords with golden tassels [that] sustain two or three hundred magnificently bound books." But books should not be primly confined to bookcases. With a little stretch of the imagination, you can find some very inventive ways to keep books close at hand. They can always be piled on side chairs or on a footstool near your favorite easy chair. Set small stacks of them on staircases, along the wall, or on an expanse of desk. A group of books in a basket left on a bedside table in the guest room is a thoughtful gesture.

Since the invention of the printing press and movable type in the fifteenth century, books have been treasured. And books on every subject—from architecture to zoology—have been collected by all sorts of people, including emperors and kings. Thomas Jefferson had one of the finest libraries in colonial America, and John Pierpont Morgan's extraordinary collection today is open to the public in a wonderful small museum, the Pierpont Morgan Library, in New York City.

In the past, such famous collectors had the wherewithal to find and purchase rare books that would be impossible for most of us today because of dwindling supply. Prices have risen higher and higher as books have appreciated. However, there are still many delights to be found and enjoyed. I love to escape from the cares of daily life by visiting old bookstores and collecting herbals and old gardening books filled with lavish engravings and gardening

Previous page: *Books belong in every room—a market basket filled with Victorian volumes in a guest room.*
Above left: *L'Europe, a hand-colored engraving, made in France about 1830.*
Right: *In an old family library a Venetian blackamoor stands behind a volume of Boydell's* Shakespeare Gallery, *1803, which is filled with engravings. An ivory paper cutter marks the place.*

ideas that are still timely.

Almost always, the books you buy should be in good condition. But as we know with antiques, there are no absolute rules. Recently, for example, an 1827 copy of *Tamerlane* by Edgar Allan Poe, in only fair condition, was found in a New Hampshire barn. One of only twelve known copies, it was purchased for $15 and auctioned for $198,000 shortly after. Obviously, the rarity here outweighed any other factor.

One of my best-loved books as a child was *The Wind in the Willows* by Kenneth Grahame. There are delightful descriptions of the animals' cozy homes, including Mole's snug cottage, where Ratty exclaims, "This is really the jolliest little place I ever was in. Now, wherever did you pick up those prints? Make the place look so homelike, they do." Prints do make a room look warm and inviting. Evelyn Kraus, the co-owner of Ursus Books and Prints in New York, recently told me,

"Old prints, made on old paper with old coloring, create an instant ambience of inherited patina in any room."

Peter Thornton's *Authentic Decor: The Domestic Interior* comprises three centuries of valuable ideas for decorating a room with drawings, watercolors, and, especially, prints. A grouping of gilt frames the same size has symmetry and calm, while an assortment of antique frames of various sizes, from different pe-

Left: *Embossed and gilt leather has a mellow richness. A battle scene is engraved on a leather and paper wallet, made in the early 19th century.*
Above: The Historie of Foure-Footed Beastes, *printed in 1607 by William Jaggard with engravings of exotic animals, is one of the earliest natural history books.*
Overleaf: *Silhouettes surround a William IV mirror, above a pair of chestnut tôle urns.*

riods, has a more accumulated, less formal look. Other objects can be mixed in with prints—porcelain plates, for example. Small, highly visible spaces such as the entry foyer benefit from framed prints displayed there.

Old prints are like windows into other worlds. Like books, they connect us not only with the past, but with present interests as well. The availability of prints brought art to the masses, as printmakers produced inexpensive copies of great works of art.

Many of the early prints we see framed were originally made to illustrate books or portfolios of text and were never intended to be hung on walls. An architect, for example, could carry a book of building details, including designs for fireplaces, plasterwork, and doorways, as a practical way to show his work to clients in the days before photography. Designs by Andrea Palladio and architectural views by Giovanni Battista Piranesi are fine examples of portfolio leaves that we now see framed. Prints were also a way for scientists and explorers to share their newfound knowledge in botany and natural history. Maps were etched and sometimes beautifully hand-colored.

Interest in prints sometimes becomes a steppingstone to collecting watercolors and drawings from which prints were made—for example, John James Audubon's watercolors. Every collector of prints should know something about printmaking techniques. A good book on the subject is *Prints and People* by A. Hyatt Mayor, who was a renowned curator of prints at the Metropolitan Museum of Art.

Most of the old prints being collected today were made from about 1600 to 1850. The techniques most frequently used in producing the decorative prints we find so appealing include the following:

• *Woodcut* is relief printing made by cutting a block of wood with a knife along the grain. The areas that are not to print are gouged away, leaving raised lines that

are then inked and pressed onto paper. In the fifteenth century, woodcuts were used to make playing cards. And in seventeenth-century Japan, the technique reached new

Left: *Engravings and the title page from* Representation des Animaux de la Menagerie de S. A. S. Monseigneur Le Prince Eugène François de Savoye et de Piemont, *printed in 1734. The book was a record of the plants and animals in this nobleman's very unusual private zoo. With their frames touching, they hang as one big picture above a pen-work table.*

Above: *Old lithographs set in identical gold-leaf picture frames in a narrow hallway.*

heights with depictions of the restless beauty of the natural world.

• *Wood engraving* is also a kind of relief printing, but the block of wood is cut across the grain. Much finer engraving tools are used. Albrecht Dürer's extraordinary engravings first come to mind, as well as Thomas Bewick's illustrated books with exquisite little vignettes of country life in eighteenth-century England.

• *Engraving* is the cutting of lines into a sheet of copper or steel. In engraving, the line that is cut is the line that prints. Uncut areas do not print. Appearing around the same time as the woodcut, engraving evolved from the goldsmith's art.

• *Drypoint* is a kind of engraving in which the metal plate is scratched with a steel needle. It was often used in combination with etching.

• *Mezzotint*—literally "halftone"—is another kind of engraving in which different areas of the plate are scraped to produce light and shadow. Developed in the seventeenth century, it allowed printmakers to achieve a velvety background.

• *Stipple* is also an engraving technique. The metal plate is dabbed repeatedly with the point of the tool to create patterns of dots. The density of the dots affects the depth of tone achieved.

• *Etching* is the technique of using acid, instead of an engraving tool, to "bite" lines into a metal plate. As in engraving, the lines print black. Some of the finest painters, such as Rembrandt, Tiepolo, Van Dyke, Goya, Whistler, and Turner, were accomplished etchers as well.

• *Aquatint* is a kind of etching process produced by varying the amount of time different areas of the plate are exposed to the acid. The tones created resemble ink or watercolor washes. The aquatints of American Impressionist Mary Cassatt are among the most delicate ever made.

• *Lithography*, invented in the 1790s, is drawing with a grease pencil on a slab of limestone, which is then treated, wet with water, and spread with printer's ink. The ink clings to the greasy lines and is re-

Previous pages: *In the 18th century it was fashionable to have a print room. This pantry is papered with antique botanical engravings glued right to the walls and doors as they would have been then.*

Above: *Lady Georgina's bedroom at Castle Howard in York is one of the loveliest rooms of any I have visited in England. It is practically as she left it in 1858, filled with prints, drawings, and watercolors of her family and friends. An unusual four-poster bed with ivy painted on the bedposts is hung with deep yellow silk damask from about 1770. Batiste and lace pillows and bedcover complete the picture in a very cheerful room.*

Previous pages: *Arranging prints cleverly can change a room. They add a liveliness and color, especially when they depict natural subjects, such as butterflies and botanicals, or detail the fashions of times gone by. Choosing a theme—flowers in baskets, for example—can be fun. Little, seemingly unimportant pieces, once framed, become interesting additions to a wall.*

Above: *When you run out of wall space, leaning framed prints and engravings on rarely used chairs is a nice solution, as in this hallway. If you redecorate, or rearrange as much as I do, they can be changed at will, giving newness to the room. You can also do this if you are undecided—prop the print up somewhere and live with it before hanging it up.*

pelled by the water. The inked lines are then transferred to a sheet of paper pressed against the stone. In nineteenth-century America, the most prolific lithographers were Currier and Ives, who captured the flavor of the era in their prints of country life, rural landscapes, and ships.

Here are some ways in which paper has been used in the decorative arts:

• *Autographs.* This category includes letters, documents, or signatures of prominent people. It is an area in which you can become involved with the history of the person whose writings interest you.

• *Calligraphy.* In the nineteenth century, calligraphy exercises were performed by students learning penmanship. They also drew stylized lions, birds, and other creatures copied from instruction books. Some of the results are quite colorful and ornamental, like the frakturs that the Pennsylvania Germans created.

• *Collage.* Bits of colored paper were cut and pasted on a colored background to form a picture.

• *Filigree work.* Narrow strips of cut paper were rolled into spirals, which were glued to a background in patterns resembling wire filigree. You will sometimes see workboxes made of filigree work.

• *Paper cutout pictures.* Intricate patterns and pictures were cut from a single sheet of paper and then mounted on a darker one. Even prayers and quotations have been skillfully cut, almost as delicate as lace, and much more fragile.

• *Photographs.* Seemingly tangential to the other paper antiques listed here, early photography—daguerreotypes, tin types, glass plates, and so on—has become a burgeoning area of collecting. It is also one that demands an expertise that is both challenging and rewarding to acquire.

• *Pinprick pictures.* Words and pictures were drawn by the novel technique of using different-sized pins to make holes in a sheet of paper. Sometimes the picture was watercolored over the pinpricking.

• *Silhouettes.* As with miniatures, silhouettes were ordered by people to record their likenesses. Dark paper was cut out in the shape of a person's profile and pasted on a light background, or the silhouette was "hollow cut" into a sheet of white paper, which was then mounted on a black background that showed through. With the introduction of the daguerreotype, the silhouette became obsolete.

• *Wallpapers.* Fine old block-printed or hand-painted wallpapers are really works of art. Those by Jean-Baptiste Reveillon were so complicated that they sometimes required several hundred blocks to print. Like old printed textiles, they can be framed. Bandboxes also make a nice collection stacked high on the floor in a corner of the room.

Like pieces of fabric, paper is very vulnerable to damage from light, moisture, and air pollution. Condition affects the value of books, prints, and other paper antiques. When I asked Evelyn Kraus what to look for, she said, "The condition should be as close as possible to the way it was when it first appeared. That's not always going to be possible, and you do want a certain amount of age-toning, a kind of creaminess that old paper has, especially if there is a high rag content." The amount of rag in old paper also makes it thicker than new paper.

There will be watermarks in sheets made before 1800, or a grid of "laid marks," where a new sheet of paper was laid on a screen to dry. If a print came from a book, three of its edges should be slightly browner and more worn than the one that was bound into the book's spine. Prints pulled from plates should have a plate mark—an indentation where the plate was pressed into the paper.

When buying prints you should look carefully for certain things. Good condition is a must. Foxed, stained, or faded prints are not good investments. Look for fine, crisp detail and original hand-coloring, contemporary with the date of the print. Because of demand, old black-and-white

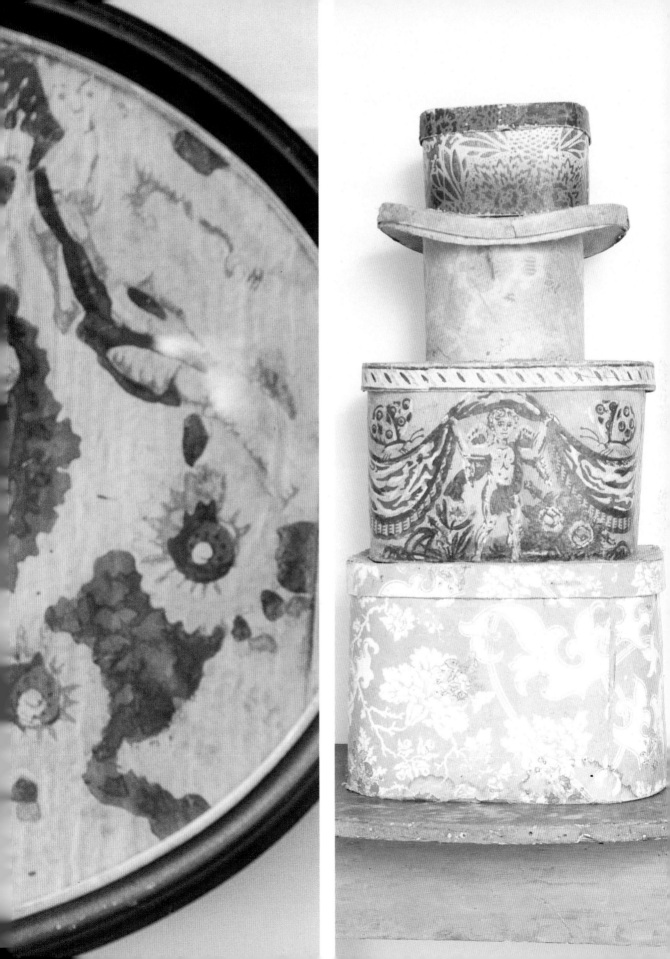

prints have sometimes been newly colored in. If you suspect this, ask the dealer, since it will affect the value of the print. To make certain that the original margins are complete and pristine, you should examine a print outside its frame.

Old paper needs special handling. Prints should be framed with acid-free liners and mats and stored in acid-free tissue, folders, or boxes. These are among the mail-order museum suppliers of special cleaning products for antiques.

- Talas, 213 West 35th Street, New York, NY 10001 (212-736-7744)
- University Products Inc., P.O. Box 101, Holyoke, MA 01041 (800-628-1912)
- The Paper Source, 8420 Porter Lane, Alexandria, VA 22308 (800-542-2270).

One of the best places to find and examine old prints and books is at specialist fairs. One of the oldest ones, the London Antiquarian Book Fair, has been an annual event for three decades. All the very best dealers in the world are clustered together under one roof. It offers an unparalleled opportunity to see thousands of objects and to meet the experts in your area.

In fact, at most fine antiques shows, you will find several dealers of prints and antiquarian books. These shows offer a dazzling cornucopia of the best in the decorative arts and are not to be missed.

The calendar of antique shows and fairs now includes not only antiquarian book, map, and print fairs, but ephemera as well. These are dedicated to all the little bits and pieces of memorabilia that capture the flavor of everyday life of the past—old trade cards, broadsides, catalogs, postcards, political material, labels.

Bits of ephemera have an irresistible graphic appeal, and they can be quite affordable. For instance, I have framed old invoices from seed companies. With engraved letterheads, they are covered with the fine Spencerian handwriting of a nineteenth-century clerk. The labels the Shakers pasted on their jars of dried herbs and

N7

GUINEVERE
LONDON

homemade tonics are miniature delights.

When you collect antiques, especially pieces of ephemera, you sometimes come across something that is relevant to the area in which you live. If you can, buy it and take it to your local historical society. It may turn out to be something that you can donate to them. Then they can research it, preserve it properly, and display it for others to enjoy.

In 1923 Howard Carter wrote in *The Discovery of the Tomb of Tutankhamen*, "The things [an archaeologist] finds are not his own property, to treat as he pleases, or neglect as he chooses. They are a direct legacy from the past to the present age, he but the privileged intermediary through whose hands they come."

While the things we find may not be as momentous as those uncovered by Carter, I do think that it is up to all of us to preserve the bits and pieces of the past that have survived if we can.

Previous pages, left: *You can sometimes find precious fragments of old woodblock-printed wallpapers that can be framed. This piece, early 19th century, becomes something very special in its own round frame.* Right: *Bandboxes and hatboxes can be stacked on a table or on the floor. These are American, from early- to mid-19th century, each one lined with dated newspapers of the period. The hat-shaped one, made for a man, is unusual.*

Above: *You can usually find prints at most large antiques shows both here and abroad. It's fun to look for old engravings, watercolors, maps, books, and other paper antiques while wandering up and down aisles that are filled with sophisticated displays of all kinds of antiques. The Burlington House Fair, the Winter Antiques Show, and the Decorative Antiques and Textiles Fair are a few attractive shows.*

Overleaf: *An old-fashioned bulletin board holds evocative bits and pieces of ephemera from the past.*

The Care and Handling of Paper

Works on Paper

Works on paper are fragile. Properly handled and stored, however, they can last a very long time indeed.

- Old prints and documents should be handled as little and as gently as possible. Never pick up a work on paper by the tips of your fingers. The weight of the paper alone might be enough to cause a tear.

- Before framing or storing old paper, remove any metal things—staples and paper clips—from it. These can be disastrous, leaving rust spots and making holes where they've been attached.

- When storing prints and other flat papers, keep them in acid-free folders and in acid-free boxes. See the listing on page 180 for where to buy these supplies. Never store anything in any room that undergoes wide fluctuations of temperature and humidity. Dry heat especially dries out paper.

- When framing, remember that any paper that touches an old print should be acid-free. In the case of a framed print, this means an acid-free mat and backing. You may acquire a print that is already nicely framed. Rather than discard the frame, you can have an acid-free liner inserted between the mat and the print and have an acid-free backing added. This will protect your print.

- Be aware that strong light causes the greatest damage to paper—colors fade and paper dries out. If the room is unavoidably bright, prints should be framed with ultraviolet-proof Plexiglas. Choose incandescent rather than fluorescent light. Position things out of direct light, if possible.

- Personally, I do not find a little foxing on an old print to be unattractive. But if you do feel that a print needs to be cleaned or restored, take it to a paper conservator. Old papers were handmade and their quality is very uneven. In many cases only an expert will be able to determine their composition.

Books

- *Always* remove a book from the shelf to dust it. This may sound obvious, but a surprising number of people just run a dustcloth or even a vacuum over the tops of books that are still on the shelf. Old leather bindings tend to become dry and rip very easily. When you're taking a book down off a bookshelf, whether to clean or consult it, always try first to push the book out a little bit. With the book jutting out slightly from the shelf, you'll be able to get a good grip on it with your whole hand.

- When dusting, hold the book in your hands very firmly, its spine upward, keeping it closed so that the dust doesn't seep in between the pages. Then gently dust the top of the leaves where the dirt has settled. The brush you use on your books should be reserved for that job alone. Once you've dusted a volume, it can be reshelved. Never pack books together tightly. Crowding can damage bindings.

- We've all tucked newspaper clippings into books. Newsprint, however, has a high acid content, and this will slowly destroy the book pages it touches. Also, while it's tempting (very) to press flowers between the leaves of a book, remember that they will damage the fibers of the paper pages.

- Be aware of the humidity and temperature levels of the room where your books are kept. Too much humidity leads to mold and mildew; too little, to brittleness. The ideal humidity range is between 55 and 65 percent. The ideal temperature is between 60° and 70° F.

CHAPTER VII

A PERSONAL VIEW

People occasionally ask me how I became such an enthusiastic collector. There is no simple answer to that. What motivates anyone to collect? Sometimes it begins with one or two precious objects inherited from a relative— family silver, a delicate lace fan bought long ago on a grand tour, or a christening gown passed down from one child to another. An old family home, lived in for generations, yields up its treasures to those who are curious enough to explore. Or a simple yearning to be surrounded by things of beauty prompts a desire to reach back to the past to create something that seems more stable or lasting.

In one of his many books, Edmond de Goncourt, the writer and important nineteenth-century collector, wrote of his Sunday forays as a boy with his aunt to the antiques shops of Paris in the 1830s. He describes her as "one of the four or five people in Paris who had a passion for old things, for what was deemed beautiful in bygone ages, for Venetian glass, carved ivory, marquetry furniture, point d'Alençon lace and Dresden china. . . . It is those far-off Sundays that have made of me the collector of bibelots I have been and still am, and will remain all of my life."

The impulse to collect often begins in childhood. Some children are natural collectors, their pockets always filled with objects they cannot be parted from. I have been a hoarder ever since I was little. People always brought me things and I invariably treasured them. In fact, as I look around, I find that I still have some of them. Our nieces and nephews accumulate masses of things every summer— from crystals and geodes to little antiques found in antiques shows, to perfect birds' nests found on the ground in our meadow. They scan the world around them and find such delights. Perhaps it runs in the family, and with this beginning they will no doubt become collectors as adults.

For some people it doesn't matter whether the objects come from a thrift shop or tag sale or from a pristine curio cabinet in a very posh antiques store. Most collectors say that they will buy anything if they can afford it, and sometimes even if they cannot. Being that passionate about something, being willing to sacrifice for it, is all part of collecting.

Other people take a more cerebral approach, reflecting a scholar's love of research and reason. The parameters of their collections are carefully defined, and objects are carefully chosen and edited. They can be ruthless in their discipline— "We only collect with a definite purpose in mind," say some—but no less passionate about the results.

For many of us, the rewards of collecting are much simpler. Once, an inveterate antiques buff said, "I like to pop into antiques shops and refresh myself." That may sound peculiar to some, but I think it's very true for others. It's sometimes relaxing just to look at something and enjoy the simple fact of its beauty. The longer you look, the more complex it becomes. The search never ends. One thing leads to another in an unbroken procession until you begin to wonder whether the things you collect aren't really collecting you. This pastime can, if not take over part of your life, certainly influence it.

Whether you live in a studio apartment or a mansion, the collecting impulse can give a lifetime of pleasure. I just read in a magazine the other day about an Ital-

Previous pages: *Brass hands rest on the marble bases of these late 19th-century cornucopia-shaped glass vases.*
Above left: *Hand and Heart is the subject of an American paper valentine. Made in the 19th century, it was found in an old scrapbook at a country fair.*
Right: *A collection of hands, on brass paper clips, clear satin-glass vases, and a milk-glass trinket dish, surrounded by Victorian linen and lace.*

featuring only advertising tins and tin boxes.

Collectors are always projecting. What unwanted object today will be sought after tomorrow? To find something you love that no one else cares much about is a wonderful, offbeat way to collect. Andy Warhol amassed a sizable collection of cookie jars, long overlooked. And in the 1920s and '30s, few inspired collectors recognized the value of American folk art. Abby Aldrich Rockefeller and Henry Francis du Pont led the way and started museums to preserve our heritage. We owe them a big thank you for their curiosity and farsightedness.

Many areas are still awaiting discovery. Today, however, a new sophistication permeates the collector's world. The beauties of the past are both irreplaceable and essential, and more and more people realize that everything deserves a second look. As a result, competition, always a factor, has intensified.

In photographing for this book, we went from tiny city apartments to enormous castles in the country. The people we met were gracious and delightful, and all had something in common: they loved beautiful things and were infectiously enthusiastic about them. They shared their knowledge avidly, whether it was small, quirky antiques or elegant, dignified objects that they collected.

As these photographs show, there are endless ways of living with the objects you collect. In times long past there were curio rooms in which the nobility displayed

ian principessa with fifteen generations of collectors behind her. She has been adding to the vast inherited collection for decades and said, "There is hardly a day when I don't discover and bring home some new treasure." She looks everywhere—from prestigious European showrooms to stalls in the flea markets.

A collection usually reflects the personality of the person behind it. If two people collect the same thing—china, for example—their collections will probably look very different. Each is based on the individual's taste, style, experience, background, and the intangibles of soul and heart. The things you don't buy are as telling as those you do.

Opportunity can also influence what you collect. I started accumulating Huntley and Palmer biscuit tins when there were lots around. I was intrigued by their varied shapes and graphic design and collected them until I couldn't afford to anymore. Now you can go to special auctions

Above left: A unique collection of English silver and silver parcel-gilt spice boxes, scent bottles, and pomanders dating from the 16th to the 18th centuries.
Above right: Old frames mixed with new ones. Antique frames always make photographs look more distinctive.
Right: Bronze animals, collected since the owner was a little girl, romp on a handmade drawnwork teacloth. The pillows are cross-stitched in the old Russian style.

the curiosities and artifacts found on travels abroad. Today few of us can spare a separate room, and in any event we try to make our antiques a part of day-to-day living.

Garvin Mecking, whose antiques store in New York City bears his name and has great style and individuality, once told me, "What I enjoy most about collecting is, truthfully, to have such a quantity of objects that I can put some away, as the Japanese do, and then bring them back out again later. A collection is always fun when it's exciting, and it's exciting for me only when it's new. Putting things away for a time renews them. There's a drawer in the shop where I keep ivory this way, and I have some dishes at home that I don't even see for two or three years at a time. Then I have a dinner party and bring them out and use them. They're new all over again, and I like them as well as when I first saw them."

A collection that is a great mishmash of objects of all periods and purposes can still have tremendous fascination and appeal. It is held together by the affection and taste of the person or family who formed it. The layers and layers of objects look at home together, and harmony between objects in a home is important. If chosen with care, the objects fit together, like a patchwork quilt, now coordinating, now contrasting. A house filled with fine old things, personal mementos, lots of

books, and fresh flowers from the garden is my idea of home. A very special book in which these themes are explored is John Cornforth's book on taste and interior decoration, *The Inspiration of the Past.*

Having a strong, confident point of view has been a mark of the very best collectors since the beginning of time. Fortunately for us, many of these people, having amassed enormous collections, then started their own museums. In some cases, their families preserved their collections intact, donating them to a single museum. Following is a list of museums

Left: *Christmas gifts, given by a couple to each other over the years, include a rare, 19th-century carved wood architect's model for a staircase. It is surrounded by a group of carefully chosen desk accessories, including agate and marble paperweights, books, and rulers.*
Above: *A collection of scent bottles, old and new, was begun with one given to the owner by her godmother. It now includes souvenirs of trips and happy occasions. Starting someone on a collection, or adding to it, is wonderful.*
Overleaf: *Red, red, red. This happy color becomes the basis for a collection, a delightful idea. The child's red tartan dress, about 1880, lends a whimsical feeling to this unusual arrangement, which includes stacks of bright red books.*

Discovering new areas of collecting is a way to make your personal collections unique. It's exciting to look for and buy (at reasonable prices, usually) objects that few are interested in yet.

Above: These detailed greeting cards are 19th-century Austrian. With their intricate embossed designs and elaborate gold borders, each one makes a little picture framed within the whole.

Left: An interest in seashells found expression in a tiered shellwork table that now creates a grotto effect in a hallway. In the 18th and 19th centuries, real shells were glued in patterns to a variety of objects, especially boxes with lids, such as those seen here. They could be used for jewelry or keepsakes.

Right: Hand-painted and stenciled fire fans were hung on a door by a collector pressed for space, a clever solution with sophisticated results. Originally, these fans were held in the hand to protect the face when sitting near the fireplace.

that I particularly like. I have tried to highlight those with remarkable or extensive collections of decorative arts. The Walters Art Gallery in Baltimore, the Huntington Library in California, the Ca'Rezzonico in Venice, and the Forbes Magazine Galleries in New York are examples of such museums. They each have a definite focus and personal slant that appeals to me. Because most are just off the beaten track, they are rarely very crowded, and one can look and enjoy in a quiet atmosphere.

I also like to visit museums, such as Sir John Soane's Museum in London, that were originally private homes. It affords an opportunity to catch a glimpse of the spirit behind the collection. I was recently leafing through *An Illustrated History of Interior Decoration* by Mario Praz and found something lovely that he wrote about it in the 1940s: "For houses I have a special weakness. It's not only that I find myself more in touch with the past: the

very arrangement of the furnishings acts on me like a spell. The odor of the furniture, of the wax on the floors, of the ancient rooms is as pleasing to me—or even more pleasing—than the scent of meadows in spring. . . . Of the many apartments I visited in former times how many can still be traced today? At the end of the Second World War, I wondered if the classic house of Sir John Soane still stood in a vast, grey London square with its melancholy, fenced-in garden. That house as still as a tomb, at the bottom of a sea of fog . . . that house which has the air of a museum and of a catacomb with busts, sarcophagi, urns, bas-reliefs, red and black Greek vases, furniture of dark mahogany, smoky ceiling paintings. . . ."

Happily, the house was and is still there. Sir John Soane, the distinguished architect and consummate collector, not only bought such great works as Hogarth's *The Rake's Progress,* but also had the vision to purchase from the Adam family

A special collection can have great appeal. There is also the charm of pursuing a single theme.

Above left: *Staffordshire pottery hens nesting on shelves, each one delightfully different. The owner has collected them all her life and uses them when entertaining.*

Above center: *Miniature hats to suit every occasion. Some are pottery, others glass, silver, or brass. The owner, a teen-ager now, began to accumulate these when he was a boy in grade school. Friends and family, intrigued with so young a collector, are always on the lookout for hats to add.*

Above right: *English spaniels from the 19th century, looking very alert. Made in earthenware, each one was hand-painted, so no two are alike. They were made in all sizes, from miniature to almost life size, usually in facing pairs that could be displayed on shelves and fireplace mantels. Today, the owner has them tucked into every nook and corner of her lovely home, a friendly and personal touch.*

Overleaf: *Several glimpses inside Sir John Soane's Museum in Lincoln's Inn Fields, London, including,* clockwise from left:

A bust of Inigo Jones, foremost British architect of the 17th century, sits within a narrow loggia that runs along the front of the building facing a stately square.

The breakfast room, with its unusual domed ceiling, corner mirrors, and view across the court, is characteristic of Soane's unique architectural style.

A bust of Soane sits among ancient plaster casts of sculpture, urns, and busts in the oldest part of the house. The famous sarcophagus of Seti I (1303–1290 B.C.) is also located here.

Soane's serene private office, filled with watery light, is hung with architectural fragments of friezes and cornices over the long drafting tables.

Sulfur casts from gems by Nathaniel Marchant are tucked into a corner of a narrow hallway with windows.

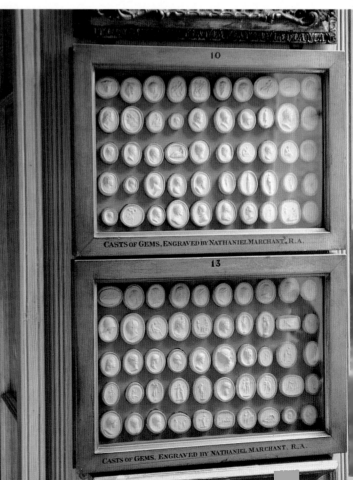

CASTS OF GEMS, ENGRAVED BY NATHANIEL MARCHANT. R.A.

CASTS OF GEMS, ENGRAVED BY NATHANIEL MARCHANT. R.A.

fifty-three volumes of original architectural drawings by the brothers Robert and James Adam. The house was established as a museum in 1833 while Soane was still alive, and he directed that it be maintained just as he left it.

In England and France, there are numerous historic homes, many still lived in by their owners, that are open to the public. I have included the names and addresses of several organizations that can furnish you with lists of them.

In the United States, almost every city and many small towns have a historical society. They often house antique treasures donated by notable, old local families. Be sure not to miss visiting them when you travel. They add a human dimension to museum-going.

Visiting the Forbes Magazine Galleries in New York City is a memorable museum experience. The displays are exciting and very cleverly designed. My favorite room is the one filled with extraordinary Fabergé masterpieces.

Left: Breathtaking objects by Fabergé, including a revolving imperial frame of Bowenite and silver gilt. It holds informal photographs of the Russian, Danish, British, and Greek royal families. A blowup of a photograph of the Dowager Empress, Marie Feodorovna, taken after the 1917 Russian Revolution, includes this same frame.

Left: A lovely miniature of Thomas Jefferson's bedroom/study at Monticello, made by Eugene Kupjack for the Forbes Galleries. You can learn so much by visiting Jefferson's beautiful home and gardens.

HISTORIC HOUSES

UNITED STATES

The National Trust is one of the largest organizations dedicated to preserving old and historic buildings in this country.

National Trust for Historic Preservation
1785 Massachusetts Avenue, N.W.
Washington, D.C. 20036
(202) 673-4129

GREAT BRITAIN

Historic homes and stately country houses of the British Isles are filled with treasures dating from medieval times to the early twentieth century. They are showcases of the finest architecture and art. Castle Howard, Hardwick Hall, Wilton, Chatsworth, and Knole are but a few I recommend.

Country Houses Association Limited
41 Kingsway
London WC2
(01) 836-1624

English Heritage
P.O. Box 43, South Ruislip
Middlesex
(01) 845-7788

Historic Houses Association
38 Ebury Street
London SW1
(01) 730-9419

The National Trust
36 Queen Anne's Gate
London SW1
(01) 222-9251

Treasure Houses of England
Bedford Estates
29A Montague Street
London WC1
(01) 636-2713

AUSTRALIA

There are many houses open to the public in Australia; some also offer accommodation. Write to the National Trust in your state, or

Australian Council of National Trusts
P.O. Box 1002
Civic Square ACT 2608
(062) 476 766

NEW ZEALAND

New Zealand Historic Places Trust
P.O. Box 2629
Wellington NZ
(04) 724 341

FRANCE

Over one thousand châteaus are open to the public in France. Some take overnight guests. They aptly record France's contribution to decorative and fine arts and to the art of living. I especially like Chenonçeaux, Mont Geoffroy, Maintenon, Blois, and, of course, Versailles.

Caisse Nationale des Monuments Historiques et des Sites
Hôtel de Sully
62 rue Saint-Antoine
Paris, France 75004
(1) 42-74-22-22

La Demeure Historique
55 Quai de la Tournelle
Paris, France 75005
(1) 43-29-028

MUSEUMS

UNITED STATES
California

Los Angeles County Museum of Art
5905 Wilshire Boulevard
Los Angeles, CA 90036
(213) 857-6111

The J. Paul Getty Museum
17985 Pacific Coast Highway
Malibu, CA 90265
(213) 458-2003

District of Columbia

National Gallery of Art/ Smithsonian
4th Street and Constitution
    Avenue, N.W.
Washington, DC 20560
(202) 737-4215

National Museum of American History/Smithsonian
4th Street and Constitution
    Avenue, N.W.
Washington, DC 20560
(202) 357-2700

The Phillips Collection
1600-1612 21 Street, N.W.
Washington, DC 20009
(202) 387-2151

Renwick Gallery/Smithsonian
17th Street and Pennsylvania
    Avenue, N.W.
Washington, DC 20560
(202) 357-2700

Maryland

Baltimore Museum of Art
Art Museum Drive
(Off Charles and 31st Street)
Baltimore, MD 21218
(301) 396-7101

Walters Art Gallery
600 North Charles Street
Baltimore, MD 21201
(301) 547-9000

Massachusetts

The Boston Athenaeum
10½ Beacon Street
Boston, MA 02108
(617) 227-0270

Isabella Stewart Gardner Museum
280 The Fenway
Boston, MA 02115
(617) 566-1401

Museum of Fine Arts
465 Huntington Avenue
Boston, MA 02115
(617) 267-9300

The Society for the Preservation of New England Antiquities, Harrison Gray Otis House
141 Cambridge Street
Boston, MA 02114
(617) 227-3956

Fogg Art Museum
32 Quincy Street
Cambridge, MA 02138
(617) 495-1910

New York

Brooklyn Museum
200 Eastern Parkway
Brooklyn, NY 11238
(718) 638-5000

The Corning Museum of Glass
One Museum Way
Corning, NY 14830
(607) 255-6464

Cooper-Hewitt Museum/ Smithsonian
2 East 91 Street
New York, NY 10128
(212) 860-6898

The Frick Collection
10 East 71 Street
New York, NY 10021
(212) 288-0700

The Metropolitan Museum of Art
Fifth Avenue at 82 Street
New York, NY 10028
(212) 535-7710

The Pierpont Morgan Library
29 East 36 Street
New York, NY 10016
(212) 685-0610

National Academy of Design
1083 Fifth Avenue
New York, NY 10128
(212) 369-4880

Pennsylvania

Philadelphia Museum of Art
Benjamin Franklin Pkwy. at 26th St.
Philadelphia, PA 19130
(215) 763-8100

GREAT BRITAIN

The American Museum in Britain
Claverton Manor
Bath
(0225) 60503

The Museum of Costume
Assembly Rooms
Bath
(0225) 61111

Number 1 Royal Crescent
Bath
(0225) 28126

Museum of Childhood
Hyndford's Close
38 High Street
Edinburgh
(031) 225-2424

Royal Scottish Museum
Chambers Street
Edinburgh
(031) 225-7534

Bethnal Green Museum
Cambridge Heath Road
London E2
(01) 980-2415

British Museum
Great Russell Street
London WC1
(01) 636-1555

Geffrye Museum
Kingsland Road
London E2
(01) 739-8368

Kensington Palace, State Apartments
Kensington Gardens
London W8
(01) 937-9561

National Gallery
Trafalgar Square
London WC2
(01) 839-3321

Sir John Soane's Museum
13 Lincoln's Inn Fields
London WC2
(01) 405-2107

Victoria and Albert Museum
Cromwell Road
London SW7
(01) 589-6371

Wallace Collection
Hertford House
Manchester Square
London W1
(01) 935-0687

Paisley Museum
High Street
Paisley
(041) 889-3151

AUSTRALIA
New South Wales

Art Gallery of NSW
The Domain
Art Gallery Road
Sydney NSW
(02) 225 1700

Powerhouse Museum
500 Harris Street
Ultimo NSW
(02) 217 0111

Sydney Textile Museum
172 St. John's Road
Glebe NSW
(02) 692 0723

Vaucluse House
Olola Avenue
Vaucluse NSW
(02) 337 1957

Elizabeth Bay House
7 Onslow Avenue
Elizabeth Bay NSW
(02) 358 2344

**Old Government House
(National Trust)**
Parramatta Park
Parramatta NSW
(02) 635 8149

Victoria

Victorian Arts Centre
St. Kilda Road
Melbourne VIC 3004
(03) 617 8263

Johnson Collection
(largest collection of decorative arts
in Australia)
contact: Rodney Davidson
(03) 654 3455

Museum of Victoria
328 Swanston Street
Melbourne VIC
(03) 669 9888

Como House (National Trust)
Como Avenue
South Yarra VIC 3141
(03) 241 2500

South Australia

Art Gallery of South Australia
North Terrace
Adelaide SA 5000
(08) 223 7200

Ayers House (National Trust)
288 North Terrace
Adelaide SA 5000
(08) 223 1655

Old Government House
Belair National Park
Belair SA 5052
(08) 278 5477

Martindale Hall
(also offers accommodation)
Mintaro SA 5415
(08) 843 9011

Western Australia

**Woodbridge House (National
Trust)**
3 Third Avenue
West Midland WA 6056
(09) 274 2432

**Old Farm Strawberry Hill
(National Trust)**
17 Beauchamp Street
Albany WA 6330
(09) 841 3735

Samson House
Ellen Street & Hampton Road
Fremantle WA 6160
(09) 335 2553

Hall Collection Museum
105 Swan Street
Guildford WA 6055
(09) 279 6579

Queensland

Queensland Art Gallery
Queensland Culture Centre
South Brisbane QLD 4101
(07) 840 7333/7303

Tasmania

Clarendon (National Trust)
Nile
Evandale TAS 7212
(003) 98 6220

Entally House (National Trust)
Hadspen TAS 7257
(003) 93 6201

The White House
(Staffordshire pottery and oak
furniture)
Village Green
Westbury TAS 7303
(ring National Trust for information)

**Tasmanian Museum and Art
Gallery**
40 Macquarie Street
Hobart TAS 7000
(002) 23 1422

ACT

Australian National Gallery
Parkes Place
Parkes ACT 2600
(062) 71 2502

NEW ZEALAND

Auckland Museum
Auckland

National Museum
Wellington

Canterbury Museum
Christchurch

Otago Museum
Dunedin

FRANCE

**Musée National Adrien
Dubouché**
8 bis Place Winston Churchill
Limoges, France 87000
(55) 77-45-58

Musée des Arts Décoratifs
30-32 rue de la Charité
Lyon, France 69001
(7) 837-15-05

Musée Historique de Tissus
34 rue de la Charité
Lyon, France 69002
(7) 837-15-05

Musée de l'Impression sur Étoffes
3 rue des Bonnes-Gens
Mulhouse, France 68100
(89) 45-51-20

Musée Cognacq-Jay
23 Boulevard des Capucines
Paris, France 75002
(1) 47-42-94-71

Musée de Cluny
6 Place Paul-Painlevé
Paris, France 75005
(1) 43-25-62-00

Musée de la Chasse et de la Nature
60 rue des Archives
Paris, France 75003
(1) 42-72-86-43

Musée de la Mode et du Costume
Palais Galliera
10 Avenue Pierre-de-Serbie
Paris, France 75116
(1) 42-60-32-14

Musée des Arts Décoratifs
107 rue de Rivoli
Paris, France 75001
(1) 42-60-32-14

Musée d'Orsay
9 Quai Anatole France
Paris, France 75007
(1) 45-44-41-85

Musée Jacquemart-André
158 Boulevard Haussmann
Paris, France 75008
(1) 45-62-39-94

Musée Nissim de Camondo
63 rue de Monçeau
Paris, France 75008
(1) 45-63-26-32

Palais du Louvre
Rue de Rivoli
Paris, France 75003
(1) 42-60-39-26

Musée du Papier Peint
28 rue Zuber
Rixheim, France
(89) 64-24-56

Musée National de Céramique
4 Grande Rue
Sèvres, France
(1) 534-99-05

ITALY

Bargello
4 Via del Proconsolo
Florence, Italy 50122
(055) 210-801

Chiostri di Santa Maria Novella
Piazza Santa Maria Novella
Florence, Italy 50123
(055) 282-187

Galleria del Costume
Palazzo Pitti
Florence, Italy 50125
(055) 294-279

Museo Archeologico di Firenze
36 Via della Colonna
Florence, Italy 50121
(055) 247-8641

Museo Bardini e Galleria Corsi
Piazza de' Mozzi
Florence, Italy 50125
(055) 296-749

Museo degli Argenti
Palazzo Pitti
Florence, Italy 50125
(055) 212-557

Museo Horne
6 Via de' Benci
Florence, Italy 50122
(055) 244-661

Museo Stibbert
26 Via Federigo Stibbert
Florence, Italy 50134
(055) 475-520

Palazzo Davanzati
13 Via Porto Rossa
Florence, Italy 50123
(055) 216-518

Museo d'Arte Antichità
Piazza Castello
Milan, Italy 20121
(02) 808-623

Pinacoteca di Brera
28 Via Brera
Milan, Italy 20121
(02) 808-387

Poldi-Pezzoli Museum
12 Via Manzoni
Milan, Italy 20121
(02) 749-889

Borghese Gallery
Villa Borghese Gardens
Villa Umberto I
Rome, Italy 00197
(06) 858-577

Capitoline Museums
Piazza del Campidoglio
Rome, Italy 00186
(06) 678-2862

Galleria Nazionale
13 Via Quattro Fontane
Rome, Italy 00186
(06) 475-4591

Ca' Rezzonico
Grand Canal
  Dorsoduro
Venice, Italy 30124
(041) 24-543

Galleria dell'Accademia
Campo della Carità
  Dorsoduro
Venice, Italy 30124
(041) 22-247

Museo Vetrario de Murano
Fondamenta Giustiniana
  Murano
Venice, Italy 30124
(041) 739-586

Scuola di Merletti di Burano
Piazza Baldassare Galuppi
  Burano
Venice, Italy 30124
(041) 730-034

Right: *A cabinet containing the ultimate personal collection—one of everything!*

CHAPTER VIII

THE COLLECTOR'S WORLD

Not long ago, at a small country auction in England, someone purchased a dusty old painting for several hundred pounds. You might think there's nothing unusual about this, but the painting turned out to be by Canaletto, and the buyer subsequently sold it for almost $1 million. Of course, it's not every day that a forgotten work by an old master surfaces, but there are still treasures to be found if you know what you are looking for and where to look. In this chapter you'll find out where to go to learn, to look, and to buy.

You should be both knowledgeable and adventurous if you are serious about collecting. Every collector is part explorer. Each day is different in the vast world of antiques—you just never know what unexpected objects you will find, what uncharted territory you will cover.

As exciting as all this can be, it's also very hard work. I recently came across an interview with a collector who said that, contrary to what most people may think, collecting is far from a casual pastime. He put in long hours in pursuit and research, and though his feet may have wearied, his enthusiasm never flagged. I think that's true of every collector.

To smooth your way, here are some tips that I've found very helpful over the years—from setting out in the morning, to negotiating, to getting myself and my treasures home all in one piece.

Plan your day like a general in the midst of a campaign, and get yourself geared up for battle.

Dress comfortably. It's especially important to wear comfortable shoes, because you'll be on your feet much of the day. For outdoor markets, or indoor ones in winter, dress warmly. I have no tolerance for the cold, so I always tie an extra sweater around my coat. In summer, I bring a straw hat for very sunny days.

Clean out your handbag. You don't want to start off encumbered by every-thing you own. You'll be loaded down before you know it. Take your credit cards along if you are going to shops, but you will probably not be able to use them if you are going to an antiques show or market. In any event, shows and markets can be very crowded, and you don't want to have to worry about your valuables.

Make a point of getting to antiques shows early, when everything is still very fresh and there's an edge to the excitement. So much is happening at once— people streaming in, shouting greetings, haggling, buying, selling. Everything is going at a fast clip. By the end of the day this buoyant atmosphere dissipates as people tire out.

Some American shows have an early admission. For a fee, you can come onto the grounds and look before the gates are opened to the general public. Very often, dealers, collectors, and those of us who are afraid of missing anything will take advantage of this. I once found a Fortuny dress this way, proving the old adage about early birds. Even without early admission, it's still a good idea to get to the show just at opening time. There will always be plenty to choose from then.

Another good reason to arrive early is to find a parking place close to the gates. Having the car handy allows you to leave your packages there as they accumulate

Previous page: *Antiques centers are becoming increasingly popular in the United States. A group of dealers have permanent booths within the same large space, which offers great variety to the browser. This one of several in Millbrook, New York, has almost fifty dealers in it.*
Above left: *A roadside sign in Maine which, like similar signs around the world, will always cause me to stop.*
Right: *Unpacking what you've bought after an antiques show is fun. This coin silver pitcher, about 1830, was a fortuitous discovery, as it has my initial on it!*

so you don't have to carry them around with you all day. It also makes a handy retreat for a minute's rest every so often. After twenty years of going to summer antiques shows, my husband, Mel, sometimes prefers to spend a quiet hour or so in the car, reading the morning papers and just keeping an eye on things in general, while I scout the show. There are many other practical things you can do to make the most of the day.

Bring along something to eat. At most places, there will be a snack counter or stand where you can get something basic to eat. However, if you are particular, you may be disappointed. I always tuck a piece of fruit and some cookies or cheese into my tote to sustain me. Bringing a little snack also saves precious time, better spent hunting than standing in line.

If you're going to a country auction or market, make a day of it. Bring a picnic lunch and invite some friends. Meeting at lunchtime to compare notes and share treasures is wonderful fun.

Always be sure to get a receipt with your purchases. This is something you should remember to do, especially at a foreign market or outdoor antique show, where things are more informal and you may forget. You will need a receipt with a description of the object, value, and approximate date that it was made, when you go through customs. As I mentioned before, a law passed in 1930 defined an antique as anything over a hundred years old and declared that it could be brought into the United States duty free. For this reason, it's very important to have the approximate age or date of manufacture of the pieces you buy.

Hire a car if necessary. In getting to and from an antiques show or market, especially in Europe, you can't always depend on public transportation. It's sometimes worth hiring a car and driver, even for half a day. You'll then know he'll be there, ready to get you and your treasures back to the hotel. Another advantage to having a car handy is that you can leave your packages in it.

Take along several tote bags. Sometimes, as I accumulate things, I find that some kindly dealer will let me leave them with him. I can then go through the rest of the show unencumbered and start to accumulate more! In any case, always take a few totes or shopping bags. Otherwise you'll soon have your arms full and will spend more time juggling your purchases than looking for new ones.

Don't be afraid to discuss price. Negotiating prices in shops and at shows has not really been part of the American culture, but in Europe people do expect you to bargain. It can be a real education to stand in a crowded, busy market—Camden Passage in London, for example—and just open your ears and listen. I've never found it easy to bargain, but the more I've learned about antiques, the more comfortable I am talking about price. You can be very nice and matter-of-fact about it, but don't be afraid to ask. Sometimes, if a piece isn't in perfect condition, a small discount can help you to pay for the restoration. Or it can help you to pay for shipping an object home. If the price is absolutely final, the dealer will just say so. Then it's up to you to decide.

Plan to avoid problems when paying. In most local antiques stores, you can write a personal check or use a credit card. But you can't always count on this, especially out of state, at outdoor markets, or in foreign countries. I do carry checks anyway and make certain that I have proper identification. In Europe, I buy traveler's checks in the currency of the country. That way, I don't have to spend my time figuring out the exchange rates. In any case, some dealers will insist on cash or traveler's checks in their own currency. Always bring more than you need. You're almost certain to see something you must have just when you've spent your last dollar!

Arrange how to get your purchases

home. Once you're back at the hotel with your ten shopping bags, how are you going to get all these wonderful finds home? In this country, you can usually arrange with the shop to ship them for you. In Europe, if you're buying from an established store, they may have their own shipper and will help you with arrangements or recommend a very reliable shipper to you. If you are buying at an outdoor market or antiques show, it will be up to you to arrange for shipping. If you are going to Europe and know you will be doing a lot of shopping, perhaps buying a dining room table and chairs, make your contact with the shipper before you leave the States. Many of the antiques magazines and newspapers run advertisements for international shippers. Contact them and connect again when you arrive abroad. It will be that much easier if you have already laid the groundwork.

This chapter is filled with information garnered over years of traveling and collecting. Every time I look at our Victorian carpet balls, I recall the fun we had finding them. I hope your days discovering antiques will be remembered with the same pleasure in years to come. So put on your walking shoes and enjoy yourself.

ANTIQUES SHOPS AND GALLERIES

Antiques shopping is always an adventure! When in a new city, I always get the best restaurant recommendations from antiques dealers, who can be as discerning about food as they are about antiques!

The range of stores listed here runs from small, out-of-the-way shops to some of the oldest, most prestigious stores in the world. Before making a special trip to a store, always call first to find out their hours. Also listed are antiques centers where many shops congregate in a single place. Since this is a personal list of my favorites, it is concentrated in the Northeast and in those foreign cities that I tend to visit often. This personal recommendation does not extend to addresses specially added for this British/Australian edition.

There are several associations of antiques dealers, some of whom issue booklets with a list of each member store. Below are some of the finest in the United States, Canada, and England:

Art and Antique Dealers League of America
Suite 19A
353 East 78 Street
New York, NY 10021
(212) 879-7558

National Antique and Art Dealers Association of America
32 East 66 Street
New York, NY 10021
(212) 517-5760

Canadian Antique Dealers Association
P.O. Box 517, Station "K"
Toronto, Ontario
Canada M4P 2EO

British Antique Dealers Association
20 Rutland Gate
London SW7
(0386) 700-280

London and Provincial Antique Dealers' Association Limited
3 Cheval Place
London SW7
(01) 584-7911

UNITED STATES

Connecticut

Ed Clerk
Box 223, RD 1
Bethlehem, CT 06751
(203) 567-5093
    By appointment.

Nathan Liverant & Son
South Main Street
Colchester, CT 06415
(203) 537-2409

Les Trois Provinces
Route 149
Colchester, CT 06415
(203) 267-6057

Frederick I. Thaler
Cornwall Bridge, CT 06754
(203) 672-0052
    By appointment.

Deborah Witherspoon
155 Olds Kings Highway North
Darien, CT 06820
(203) 656-0127

Stephen and Carol Huber
82 Plants Dam Road
East Lyme, CT 06333
(203) 739-0772
    By appointment.

Francis Bealey
3 South Main Street
Essex, CT 06426
(203) 767-0220

Hastings House
Box 606
Essex, CT 06426
(203) 767-8217

White Farms Antiques
2 Essex Square
Essex, CT 06426
(203) 767-1876

Patty Gagarin Antiques
975 Banks North Road
Fairfield, CT 06430
(203) 259-7332 By appointment.

Le Manoir Country French Antiques
10 Sanford Street
Fairfield, CT 06430
(203) 255-1506

Lillian Blankley Cogan
22 High Street
Farmington, CT 06032
(203) 677-9259

Ruth Troiani
1 Mulberry Lane
Farmington, CT 06085
(203) 673-6191
    By appointment.

Bittersweet Antiques
Route 7
Gaylordsville, CT 06755
(203) 354-1727

The Goshen Antique Center
North Street, Route 63 North
Goshen, CT 06756
(203) 491-2320

Chelsea Antiques of Greenwich
14 West Putnam Avenue
Greenwich, CT 06830
(203) 629-2224

Georgian Antiques
382 Greenwich Avenue
Greenwich, CT 06830
(203) 625-0004

David A. Schorsch
1037 North Street
Greenwich, CT 06831
(203) 869-8797

Hobart House
Route 9A
Haddam, CT 06438
(203) 345-2015
    By appointment.

Mr. and Mrs. Jerome Blum
Ross Hill Road
Jewett City, CT 06351
(203) 376-0300
    By appointment.

Walton Antiques
Box 307
Jewett City, CT 06351
(203) 376-0862

Elizabeth S. Mankin
Main Street
Kent, CT 06757
(203) 927-3288

D. W. Linsley
Route 202, Bissell Road
Litchfield, CT 06759
(203) 567-4245

Peter Tillou Fine Art
Prospect Street
Litchfield, CT 06759
(203) 567-5706

Thomas D. and Constance Williams
Brush Hill Road
Litchfield, CT 06759
(203) 567-8794

English Heritage Antiques
13 South Avenue
New Canaan, CT 06840
(203) 966-2979

Timothy Mawson Books
Main Street
New Preston, CT 06777
(203) 868-0732

Briger Fairholme Jones
23 Old Lyme Street
Old Lyme, CT 06371
(203) 434-2467

Old Lyme Antiques
25 Lyme Street
Old Lyme, CT 06371
(203) 434-8852

Meadow Rock Farm Antiques
Route 169
Pomfret Center, CT 06259
(203) 928-7896

Canton
P.O. Box 115
Redding, CT 06875
(203) 938-9538

Buckley & Buckley
Box 736, Main Street
Salisbury, CT 06068
(203) 435-9919

Salisbury Antiques Center
Library Street
Salisbury, CT 06068
(203) 435-0424

Three Ravens Antiques
Box 677, Main Street
Salisbury, CT 06068
(203) 435-9602

Jack Anspaugh Antiques
Sherman, CT 06784
(203) 354-8227
    By appointment.

Pat Guthman Antiques
342 Pequot Avenue
Southport, CT 06490
(203) 259-5743

Avis and Rockwell Gardiner
60 Mill Road
Stamford, CT 06903
(203) 322-1129

Orkney & Yost Antiques
148 Water Street
Stonington, CT 06378
(203) 642-7226

Marguerite Riordan
8 Pearl Street
Stonington, CT 06378
(203) 535-2511
    By appointment.

Stephen Calcagni
Box 352
Washington Depot, CT 06794
(203) 868-7667

Guthman Americana
P.O. Box 392
Westport, CT 06881
(203) 259-9763

**Archives Historical
Autographs**
119 Chestnut Hill Road
Wilton, CT 06897
(203) 226-3920

**Louise Bevilacqua
Antiques**
Wilton, CT 06897
(203) 762-8458
    By appointnemt.

George Subkoff Antiques
643 Danbury Road, Route 7
Wilton, CT 06897
(203) 834-0703

British Country Antiques
50 Main Street North
Woodbury, CT 06798
(203) 263-5100

Harold E. Cole Antiques
27 Middle Quarter Road
Woodbury, CT 06798
(203) 263-4909
    By appointment.

David Dunton
Route 132 off Route 47
Woodbury, CT 06798
(203) 263-5355

Kenneth Hammitt
346 Main Street South
Woodbury, CT 06798
(203) 263-5676

Nininger & Company Gallery
Corner of Routes 6 and 47
Woodbury, CT 06798
(203) 263-5326

Delaware

Jackson-Mitchell
5728 Kennett Pike
Centreville, DE 19807
(302) 656-0110

Oak Knoll Books
214 Delaware Street
New Castle, DE 19720
(302) 328-7232

David Stockwell
3701 Kennett Pike
P.O. Box 3840
Wilmington, DE 19807
(302) 655-4466

District of Columbia

G. K. S. Bush Antiques
2828 Pennsylvania Avenue N.W.
Washington, DC 20007
(202) 965-0653

Cherishables Antiques
1608 20 Street N.W.
Washington, DC 20009
(202) 785-4087

Evans and Campbell
1214 31 Street N.W.
Washington, DC 20007
(202) 333-8448

Fleming and Meers
Hamilton Court
1228 31 Street N.W.
Washington, DC 20007
(202) 343-7777

Marston Luce
1314 31 Street N.W.
Washington, DC 20036
(202) 775-9460

Miller & Arney
1737 Wisconsin Avenue N.W.
Washington, DC 20007
(202) 338-2369

G. Randall Fine Antiques
2828 Pennsylvania Avenue N.W.
Washington, DC 20007
(202) 337-7373

Maine

Avis Howells Antiques
21 Pearl Street
Belfast, ME
(207) 338-3302

Rufus Foshee Antiques
Route 1, P.O. Box 839
Camden, ME 04843
(207) 236-2838

The Ditty Box
P.O. Box 292
Damariscotta, ME 04543
(207) 882-6618

Peter and Jean Richards
The Bristol Road, Route 130
Damariscotta, ME 04543
(207) 563-1964

**Kenneth and Paulette Tuttle
Antiques**
Box 6150, RFD 4
Gardiner, ME 04345
(207) 582-4496

Richard W. Oliver
Route 1
Kennebunk, ME 04043
(207) 985-3600

Port Antiques
Ocean Avenue
Kennebunkport, ME 04046
(207) 967-5119

Windfall Antiques
Ocean Avenue
Kennebunkport, ME 04046
(207) 967-2089

Jack Partridge
Route 1
North Edgecomb, ME 04556
(207) 882-7745

**F. O. Bailey and Joy Piscopo
Antiquarians**
141 Middle Street
Portland, ME 04101
(207) 774-1479

**Jim and Mary Alice Reilly
Antiques**
83 India Street
Portland, ME 04101
(207) 773-8815

Vose-Smith Company Antiques
646 Congress Street
Portland, ME 04102
(207) 773-6436

The Farm
Coles Hill Road
Wells, ME 04090
(207) 985-2656

R. Jorgenson Antiques
Route 1
Wells, ME 04090
(207) 646-9444

Kenneth and Ida Manko
Route 1
Wells, ME 04090
(207) 646-2595

1774 House Antiques
Route 1, RR 2
Wells, ME 04090
(207) 646-3520

Wells Union Antique Center
Route 1
Wells, ME 04090
(207) 646-3112

F. Barrie Freeman Antiques
RFD 1, Box 688
West Bath, ME 04530
(207) 442-8452

Sheila and Edwin Rideout
12 Summer Street
Wiscasset, ME 04578
(207) 882-6420

Roberta Hansen
Prince's Point
Yarmouth, ME 04096
(207) 846-4926

W. M. Schwind, Jr.
17 East Main Street
Yarmouth, ME 04096
(207) 846-9458

Maryland

Braiterman Books
20 Whitfield Road
Baltimore, MD 21210
(301) 235-4848

Crosskeys Antiques
801 North Howard Steet
Baltimore, MD 21201
(301) 728-0101

Paul Gore Hall Antiques
839 North Howard Street
Baltimore, MD 21201
(301) 462-4169

Hamilton House Antiques
891 North Howard Street
Baltimore, MD 21201
(301) 462-5218

Imperial Half Bushel
831 North Howard Street
Baltimore, MD 21201
(301) 462-1192

The Kelmscott Bookshop
32 West 25 Street
Baltimore, MD 21218
(301) 235-6810

William Blair
4839 Del Ray Avenue
Bethesda, MD 20814
(301) 654-6665

The Linen Press
P.O. Box 701
Cambridge, MD 21613
(301) 228-8858

Gary E. Young Antiques
128 South Commerce Street
Centreville, MD 21617
(301) 758-2132

Lawrence Lomax Antiques
6826 Wisconsin Avenue
Chevy Chase, MD 20815
(301) 656-1911

John C. Newcomer
32 W. Baltimore Street
Funkstown, MD 21734
(301) 790-1327

Mark Keshishian & Sons
836 Rockville Pike
Rockville, MD 20852
(301) 340-6666

Massachusetts

Don Abarbanel Antiques
East Main Street
Ashley Falls, MA 01222
(413) 229-3330

Ashley Falls Antiques
Route 7A
Ashley Falls, MA 01222
(413) 229-8759

Lewis and Wilson
Box 345, East Main Street
Ashley Falls, MA 01222
(413) 229-3330

The Vollmers
Route 7A
Ashley Falls, MA 01222
(413) 229-3463

Sage House Antiques
Route 23
Blandford, MA 01008
(413) 848-2843

James Billings
70 Charles Street
Boston, MA 02114
(617) 367-9533

Boston Antique Coop
119 Charles Street
Boston, MA 02114
(617) 227-9811

George Gravert
122 Charles Street
Boston, MA 02114
(617) 117-1593

Priscilla Juvelis Books
150 Huntington Avenue
Boston, MA 02115
(617) 424-1895

The March Hare
170 Newbury Street
Boston, MA 02116
(617) 536-7525

Nelson-Monroe Antiques
P.O. Box 8863
Boston, MA 02114
(617) 492-1368

Shreve, Crump & Low
330 Boylston Street
Boston, MA 02116
(617) 267-9100

Wenham Cross Antiques
232 Newbury Street
Boston, MA 02116
(617) 236-0409

Jerry Freeman
1429 Beacon Street
Brookline, MA 02146
(617) 731-6720

Robin Wilkerson Books
55 Reservoir Street
Cambridge, MA 02138
(617) 491-1971

Dedham Antique Shop
622 High Street
Dedham, MA 02026
(617) 329-1114

Stephen Score
159 Main Street
Essex, MA 01929
(508) 768-6252

The Herb Farm
Barnard Road
Granville, MA 01034
(413) 357-8882
    By appointment.

Paul and Susan Kleinwald
578 Main Street
Great Barrington, MA 01230
(413) 528-4252

Mullin-Jones Antiquities
525 South Main Street
Great Barrington, MA 01230
(413) 528-4871

Snyder's Store
945 South Main Street
Great Barrington, MA 01230
(413) 528-1441

Ferrell's Antiques
67A Center Street
Lee, MA 01238
(413) 243-1357

Henry B. Holt
Lee, MA 01238
(413) 243-3184
    By appointment.

Pembroke Antiques
28 Housatonic Street
Lee, MA 01238
(413) 243-1357

Charles L. Flint Antiques
81 Church Street
Lenox, MA 01240
(413) 637-1634

October Mountain Farm
136 East Street
Lenox, MA 01240
(413) 637-0439

Wayne Pratt
257 Forest Street
Marlborough, MA 01752
(617) 481-2917

Marjorie Parrott Adams
P.O. Box 117
396 Village Street
Medway, MA 02053
(617) 533-5677

Charles and Barbara Adams
15 Prospect Street
Middleboro, MA 02346
(617) 947-7277

Nina Hellman
22 Broad Street
Nantucket, MA 02554
(617) 228-4677

Herb House Antiques
New Hartford Road
Sandisfield, MA 01255
(413) 258-4847

Corner House Antiques
North Main Street
Sheffield, MA 01257
(413) 229-6627

Covered Bridge Antiques
North Main Street
Sheffield, MA 01257
(413) 229-2816

Darr Antiques & Interiors
South Main Street
(Route 7)
Sheffield, MA 01257
(413) 229-7773

Dovetail Antiques
North Main Street
Sheffield, MA 01257
(413) 229-2628

English and American Antiques
P.O. Box 741, Route 7
Sheffield, MA 01257
(413) 229-2955

Falcon Antiques
176 Undermountain Road
Sheffield, MA 01257
(413) 229-7745

Good & Hutchinson
Route 7
Sheffield, MA 01257
(413) 229-8832

1750 House Antiques
South Main Street
Sheffield, MA 01257
(413) 229-6635

Susan Silver Antiques
Route 7
Sheffield, MA 01257
(413) 229-8169

Lois W. Spring
Ashley Falls Road
Sheffield, MA 01257
(413) 229-2542

David M. Weiss Antiques
North Main Street
Sheffield, MA 01257
(413) 229-2716

Bird Cage Antiques
Route 23, P.O. Box 268
South Egremont, MA 01258
(413) 528-3556

Douglas Antiques
Route 23
South Egremont, MA 01258
(413) 528-1810

Mill Crest Antiques
Route 23
South Egremont, MA 01258
(413) 528-3027

Elliott and Grace Snyder
Box 598
South Egremont, MA 01258
(413) 528-3581

William E. Channing
Stockbridge, MA 01262
(413) 298-4971
   By appointment.

Sturbridge Antique Shops
200 Charlton Road, Route 20
Sturbridge, MA 01566
(508) 347-2744

New Hampshire

Clare Starr Antiques
34·Ledgewood Road
Bedford, NH 03102
(603) 472-3881

Carriage Barn Antiques
155 South Main Street
Franklin, NH 03235
(603) 934-6157

Ronald Bourgeault Antiques
694 Lafayette Road
Hampton, NH 03842
(603) 926-8222

Peter Sawyer Antiques
50 Moulton Ridge Road
Kensington, NH 03833
(603) 772-5279

Jeannine Dobbs Antiques
P.O. Box 1076
Merrimack, NH 03054
(603) 424-7617

Estelle M. Glavey
Route 124
New Ipswich, NH 03071
(603) 878-1200

Hayloft Antique Center
Route 4
Northwood, NH 03261
(603) 942-5153

Town Pump Antiques
RD 288, Route 4
Northwood, NH 03261
(603) 942-5515

Flag Gate Farm Antiques
Route 28
Ossipee, NH 03864
(603) 539-2231

Green Mountain Antiques Center
Route 16
Ossipee, NH 03864
(603) 539-2236

The Stuff Shop
Route 171
Ossipee, NH 03864
(603) 539-7715

The Cobbs Antiques
83 Grove Street
Peterborough, NH 03458
(603) 924-6361

Margaret Scott Carter
175 Market Street
Portsmouth, NH 03801
(603) 436-1781

Ed Weissman Antiquarian
110 Chapel Street
Portsmouth, NH 03801
(603) 431-7575

Knotty Pine Antique Market
Route 10
West Swanzey, NH 03469
(603) 352-5252

New Jersey

Fred B. Nadler Antiques
56 Mount Street
Bayhead, NJ 08742
(201) 892-2575

Harvey W. Brewer Books
P.O. Box 322
Closter, NJ 07624
(201) 768-4414

Leonard and Jacquelyn Balish
88 Lake Court
Englewood, NJ 07631
(201) 568-5385

Graymoor Antiques
P.O. Box 8127
Englewood, NJ 07631
(201) 568-1172

Carter de Holl Antiques
795 River Road
Fair Haven, NJ 07701
(201) 842-7887

Emily de Nemethy
Longview Road
Far Hills, NJ 07931
(201) 234-2340 By appointment.

Theresa and Arthur Greenblatt
P.O. Box 277
Lambertville, NJ 08530
(609) 397-1177

The People's Store Antique Center
Lambertville, NJ 08530
(609) 397-9808

Woods Edge at Sandbrook
RD 1, Box 384
Stockton, NJ 08559
(201) 788-4982

New York

John and Harriett Dow
Albany, NY 12203
(518) 449-2985
   By appointment.

Balasses House Antiques
Main Street
Amagansett, NY 11930
(516) 267-3032

Bedford Green Antiques
Village Green, Box 517
Bedford, NY 10506
(914) 234-9273

Sussex Antiques
Bedford, NY 10506
(914) 241-2919
   By appointment.

Jean Russell
Brooklyn, NY 11217
(718) 625-1604
   By appointment.

Green Willow Farm Shaker Gallery
Raup Road
Chatham, NY 12037
(518) 392-9654

The Dutch House
Route 23
Claverack, NY 12513
(518) 851-2011

N. & N. Pavlov Books & Prints
37 Oakdale Drive
Dobbs Ferry, NY 10522
(914) 693-1776

Richard and Betty Anne Rasso
Village Square
East Chatham, NY 12060
(518) 392-4501

**Toni and Sofie Stan
Antiques**
Box 151
East Norwich, NY 11732
(516) 922-7960

The Hudson Antiques Center
536 Warren Street
Hudson, NY 12534
(518) 828-9920

Hyde Park Antiques Center
184 Albany Post Road
Hyde Park, NY 12538
(914) 229-8200

Kinderhook Antique Center
Route 9H
Kinderhook, NY 12106
(518) 758-7939

Raymond B. Knight
121 Birch Hill Road
Locust Valley, NY 11560
(516) 671-7046

John Sideli Art & Antiques
Shaker Museum Road
Malden Bridge, NY 12115
(518) 766-3065

Bonner's Barn
25 Washington Street
Malone, NY 12953
(518) 483-4001

Days of Yore
Franklin Avenue
Millbrook, NY 12545
(914) 677-3244

**The Millbrook Antiques
Center**
Franklin Avenue
Millbrook, NY 12545
(914) 677-3921

Millbrook Antiques Mall
Franklin Avenue
Millbrook, NY 12545
(914) 677-9311

Tompkins Antiques
The Shunpike
Millbrook, NY 12545
(914) 677-3026
  By appointment.

Village Antique Center
Franklin Avenue
Millbrook, NY 12545
(914) 677-5160

The Wicker's Antiques
9 Partners Lane
Millbrook, NY 12545
(914) 677-3906
  By appointment.

Corinne Burke
New Paltz, NY 12561
(914) 255-1078

A La Vieille Russie
781 Fifth Avenue
New York, NY 10022
(212) 752-1727

Didier Aaron
32 East 67 Street
New York, NY 10021
(212) 988-5248

Acanthus Books
48 West 22 Street, No. 4
New York, NY 10010
(212) 463-0570

Danny Alessandro
1156 Second Avenue
New York, NY 10021
(212) 759-8210

America Hurrah Antiques
766 Madison Avenue
New York, NY 10021
(212) 535-1930

**L'Antiquaire & The
Connoisseur**
36 East 73 Street
New York, NY 10021
(212) 517-9176

The Antique Porcelain Company
112 East 71 Street
New York, NY 10021
(212) 794-9357

W. Graham Arader III
23 East 74 Street
New York, NY 10021
(212) 628-3668

Art Trading
305 East 61 Street
New York, NY 10021
(212) 752-2057

Bardith
901 Madison Avenue
New York, NY 10021
(212) 737-3775

Bardith I
1015 Madison Avenue
New York, NY 10021
(212) 737-6699

Betty Jane Bart
1225 Madison Avenue
New York, NY 10028
(212) 410-2702

Jean Paul Beaujard
209 East 76 Street
New York, NY 10021
(212) 345-8890

Bertha Black
80 Thompson Street
New York, NY 10012
(212) 966-7116

Doris Leslie Blau
15 East 57 Street
New York, NY 10022
(212) 759-3715

Vojtech Blau
800 Fifth Avenue
New York, NY 10021
(212) 249-4525

Blumka Gallery
101 East 81 Street
New York, NY 10028
(212) 734-3222

Blumka II Gallery
12 East 67 Street
New York, NY 10021
(212) 879-5611

Jutta Buck
4 East 95 Street
New York, NY 10128
(212) 289-4577
  By appointment.

Yale R. Burge
305 East 63 Street
New York, NY 10021
(212) 838-4005

Le Cadet de Gascoigne
1015 Lexington Avenue
New York, NY 10021
(212) 744-5925

Ralph M. Chait Galleries
12 East 56 Street
New York, NY 10022
(212) 758-0937

Cherchez
862 Lexington Avenue
New York, NY 10021
(212) 737-8215

The Chinese Porcelain Company
3rd Floor, 25 East 77 Street
New York, NY 10021
(212) 628-4101

Philip Colleck of London
830 Broadway
New York, NY 10003
(212) 505-2500

Randall E. Decoteau
131 West 82 Street
New York, NY 10024
(212) 362-9614
  By appointment.

Florence de Dampierre
16 East 78 Street
New York, NY 10021
(212) 734-6764

Dildarian, Inc.
595 Madison Avenue
New York, NY 10022
(212) 288-4948

Evergreen Antiques
1249 Third Avenue
New York, NY 10021
(212) 744-5664

F.D.R. Drive
109 Thompson Street
New York, NY 10012
(212) 334-0170

Richard L. Feigen
1113 East 79 Street
New York, NY 10021
(212) 628-0700

Malcolm Franklin
15 East 57 Street
New York, NY 10022
(212) 308-3344

I. Freeman & Son
12 East 52 Street
New York, NY 10022
(212) 759-6900

French and Company
17 East 65 Street
New York, NY 10021
(212) 535-3330

T. & K. French Antiques
60 Wooster Street
New York, NY 10012
(212) 219-2472

Galerie Chevalier
157 East 64 Street
New York, NY 10021
(212) 249-3922

Gem Antiques
1088 Madison Avenue
New York, NY 10028
(212) 535-7399

Vito Giallo Antiques
966 Madison Avenue
New York, NY 10021
(212) 535-9885

Price Glover
817½ Madison Avenue
New York, NY 10021
(212) 772-1740

F. Gorevic & Son
635 Madison Avenue, 2nd Floor
New York, NY 10022
(212) 753-9319

Hamilton-Hyde
413 Bleecker Street
New York, NY 10014
(212) 989-4509

Morgan Hayes Gallery
125 Christopher Street
New York, NY 10014
(212) 645-5736

Hirschl & Adler Folk Art
851 Madison Avenue
New York, NY 10021
(212) 988-FOLK

Jean Hoffman and Jana Starr Antiques
236 East 80 Street
New York, NY 10021
(212) 535-6930

Hyde Park Antiques
836 Broadway
New York, NY 10003
(212) 477-0033

James II Galleries
15 East 57 Street
New York, NY 10022
(212) 355-7040

Jean's Silversmiths
16 West 45 Street
New York, NY 10036
(212) 575-0723

Howard Kaplan Antiques
827 Broadway
New York, NY 10003
(212) 674-1000

Leo Kaplan
967 Madison Avenue
New York, NY 10021
(212) 249-6766

Kelter Malcé Antiques
361 Bleecker Street
New York, NY 10014
(212) 989-6760

Leigh Keno
19 East 74 Street
New York, NY 10021
(212) 734-2381

Kentshire Galleries
37 East 12 Street
New York, NY 10003
(212) 673-6644

Kimono House
110 West Houston Street
New York, NY 10012
(212) 966-5936

Gerald Kornblau
305 East 61 Street
New York, NY 10021
(212) 737-7433   By appointment.

Lenox Court Antiques
972 Lexington Avenue
New York, NY 10021
(212) 772-2460

Bernard and S. Dean Levy
24 East 84 Street
New York, NY 10028
(212) 628-7088

Lyme Regis
68 Thompson Street
New York, NY 10012
(212) 334-2110

Macklowe Gallery
667 Madison Avenue
New York, NY 10021
(212) 288-1124

Maison Jean-François
359 Bleecker Street
New York, NY 10014
(212) 645-4774

Malmaison
29 East 10 Street
New York, NY 10003
(212) 473-0373

Manhattan Art and Antique Center
1050 Second Avenue
New York, NY 10022
(212) 355-4400

D. M. and P. Manheim Antiques
305 East 61 Street
New York, NY 10021
(212) 535-6959
By appointment.

Joel Mathieson Antiques
190 Sixth Avenue
New York, NY 10013
(212) 966-7332

J. Mavec & Company
52 East 76 Street, 3rd Floor
New York, NY 10021
(212) 517-8822

Paul McCarron
1014 Madison Avenue
New York, NY 10021
(212) 772-1181

J. Garvin Mecking
72 East 11 Street
New York, NY 10003
(212) 677-4316

Elinor Merrell
18 East 69 Street
New York, NY 10021
(212) 288-4986
By appointment.

Ann Morris Antiques
239 East 60 Street
New York, NY 10022
(212) 755-3308

Charlotte Moss
131 East 70 Street
New York, NY 10021
(212) 772-3320

Murray Hill Antiques Center
201 East 31 Street
New York, NY 10016
(212) 686-6221

Naga Antiques
145 East 61 Street
New York, NY 10021
(212) 593-2788

Lillian Nassau
220 East 57 Street
New York, NY 10022
(212) 759-6062

Neslé
151 East 57 Street
New York, NY 10022
(212) 755-0515

Newel Art Galleries
425 East 53 Street
New York, NY 10022
(212) 758-1970

The Old Print Shop
150 Lexington Avenue
New York, NY 10016
(212) 683-3950

Old Versailles
315 East 62 Street
New York, NY 10021
(212) 421-3663

Ellen O'Neill's Supply Store
242 East 77 Street
New York, NY 10021
(212) 879-7330

Pageant Book & Print Shop
109 East 9 Street
New York, NY 10003
(212) 674-5296

Florian Papp
962 Madison Avenue
New York, NY 10021
(212) 288-6770

Susan Parrish
390 Bleecker Street
New York, NY 10014
(212) 645-5020

Pierre Deux
870 Madison Avenue
New York, NY 10021
(212) 570-9343

Place des Antiquaires
125 East 57 Street
New York, NY 10022
(212) 355-0500

Juan Portela Antiques
138 East 71 Street
New York, NY 10021
(211) 650-0085

Trevor Potts Gallery
1011 Lexington Avenue
New York, NY 10021
(212) 737-0909

Primavera Gallery
808 Madison Avenue
New York, NY 10021
(212) 288-1569

Provence Antiques
35 East 76 Street
New York, NY 10021
(212) 288-5179

Bob Pryor
1023 Lexington Avenue
New York, NY 10021
(212) 688-1516

James Robinson
15 East 57 Street
New York, NY 10022
(212) 752-6166

John Rosselli Antiques
255 East 72 Street
New York, NY 10021
(212) 737-2252

Israel Sack
15 East 57 Street
New York, NY 10022
(212) 753-6562

Charlotte F. Safir Books
1349 Lexington Avenue
New York, NY 10028
(212) 534-7933
By appointment.

Thomas Schwenke
956 Madison Avenue
New York, NY 10021
(212) 772-7222

S. J. Shrubsole
104 East 57 Street
New York, NY 10022
(212) 753-8920

Peter Speilhagen Fine Arts
372 Bleecker Street
New York, NY 10014
(212) 741-0849

Stair & Co.
942 Madison Avenue
New York, NY 10021
(212) 517-4400

Bernard Steinitz et Fils
125 East 57 Street
New York, NY 10022
(212) 832-3711

Garrick C. Stephenson
50 East 57 Street
New York, NY 10022
(212) 753-2570

M. H. Stockroom
654 Madison Avenue
New York, NY 10021
(212) 752-6696

Stubbs Rare Books & Prints
28 East 18 Street
New York, NY 10003
(212) 982-8368

Philip Suval
Box 6011
New York, NY 10022
(212) 517-8293
By appointment.

Sylvia Tearston
1053 Third Avenue
New York, NY 10021
(212) 838-0415

Lynne Tillman
12 West 83 Street
New York, NY 10024
(212) 873-3933
By appointment.

Gene Tyson Antiques
19 East 69 Street
New York, NY 10021
(212) 744-5785

Ursus Books and Prints
981 Madison Avenue
New York, NY 10021
(212) 772-8787

**Earle D. Vandekar of
Knightsbridge**
15 East 57 Street
New York, NY 10022
(212) 308-2023

Vernay & Jussel
817½ Madison Avenue
New York, NY 10021
(212) 879-3344

Frederick P. Victoria & Son
154 East 55 Street
New York, NY 10022
(212) 755-2549

Warren-Simon
374 Bleecker Street
New York, NY 10014
(212) 645-0883

Michael B. Weisbrod
987 Madison Avenue
New York, NY 10021
(212) 734-6350

Weyhe Gallery
794 Lexington Avenue
New York, NY 10021
(212) 838-5478

Whitehead & Mangan Prints
375 Bleecker Street
New York, NY 10014
(212) 242-7815

Wicker Garden
1318 Madison Avenue
New York, NY 10128
(212) 410-7000

Eli Wilner
1525 York Avenue
New York, NY 10028
(212) 744-6521

Thomas K. Woodard
835 Madison Avenue
New York, NY 10021
(212) 988-2906

S. Wyler
713 Madison Avenue
New York, NY 10021
(212) 838-1910

Kathy Schoemer
Route 116 at Keeler Lane
North Salem, NY 10560
(914) 669-8464

Somewhere In Time
Main Street
Northport, NY 11768
(516) 757-4148

Abbe and Badami
45 West Main Street
Oyster Bay, NY 11771
(516) 922-3325

Florilegium Botanical Art
Snedans Landing
Palisades, NY 10964
(914) 359-2926

**The Pawling Antique
Center**
71 Route 22
Pawling, NY 12564
(914) 855-3611

Gerry Tandy Antiques
1012 Park Street
Peekskill, NY 10566
(914) 737-1845

Vassar Antique Center
9 College View Avenue
Poughkeepsie, NY 12603
(914) 473-8260

Jonathan Trace
Peekskill Hollow Road
Putnam Valley, NY 10579
(914) 528-7963

**Beekman Arms Antique
Market**
Route 9
Rhinebeck, NY 12572
(914) 876-3477

Rhinebeck Antique Center
7 West Market Street
Rhinebeck, NY 12572
(914) 876-8168

Silhouette
15 East Market Street
Rhinebeck, NY 12572
(914) 876-4545

**Saratoga Country Antique
Center**
Route 29
Saratoga Springs, NY 12866
(518) 885-7645

Schoolhouse Antiques
West Avenue
Saratoga Springs, NY 12866
(518) 584-6296

John Keith Russell Antiques
Spring Street
South Salem, NY 10590
(914) 763-8144

Richard Camp
Montauk Highway
Wainscott, NY 11975
(516) 537-0330

De Martine's Bottle Shop Antiques
Route 44
Washington Hollow, NY 12578
(914) 677-3638

Pennsylvania

Renningers Extravaganza
Route 272
Adamstown, PA 19501
(717) 385-0104

The Carpenter's Tool Chest
401 Penn Avenue
Avondale, PA 19311
(215) 268-3488

R. Michael Roach Antiques
1026 West Lancaster Avenue
Bryn Mawr, PA 19010
(215) 527-6224

Donald R. Sack
P.O. Box 132
Buck Hill Falls, PA 18323
(717) 595-7567

James Galley
P.O. Box 187
Collegeville, PA 19426
(215) 489-2828

The Spring Mill Antique Shop
Spring Mill
Conshohocken, PA 19438
(215) 828-0205

McClees Galleries
343 West Lancaster Avenue
Haverford, PA 19041
(215) 642-1661

Jo Deane Antiques
54 West Eagle Road
Havertown, PA 19083
(215) 789-5678

Tamerlane Books
P.O. Box C
Havertown, PA 19083
(215) 449-4400

Campbell House Antiques
160 East Doe Run Road
Kennett Square, PA 19348
(215) 347-6756

Renninger's Extravaganza
Kutztown, PA 19530
(717) 385-0104

Lahaska Antique Courte
Route 202
Lahaska, PA 18931
(215) 794-7884

Harry B. Hartman Antiques
452 East Front Street
Marietta, PA 17547
(717) 426-1474

Olde Hope Antiques
Route 202
New Hope, PA 18938
(215) 862-5055

Francis J. Purcell II
88 North Main Street
New Hope, PA 18938
(215) 862-9100

Joseph Stanley
181 West Bridge Street
New Hope, PA 18938
(215) 862-9300

Louis A. Irion, III
44 North Valley Road
Paoli, PA 19301
(215) 644-7516

Bauman Rare Books
1807 Chestnut Street
Philadelphia, PA 19103
(215) 564-4274

Judith Finkel Antiques
1030 Pine Street
Philadelphia, PA 19107
(215) 923-3094

M. Finkel & Daughter
936 Pine Street
Philadelphia, PA 19107
(215) 627-7797

James and Nancy Glazer
2209 Delancey Place
Philadelphia, PA 19103
(215) 732-8788

Jansen Antiques
1036 Pine Street
Philadelphia, PA 19107
(215) 592-1670

Mel's Antiques
1233 Pine Street
Philadelphia, PA 19107
(215) 545-0436

The Philadelphia Print Shop
8441 Germantown Avenue
Philadelphia, PA 19118
(215) 242-4750

Reese's Antiques
928–30 Pine Street
Philadelphia, PA 19107
(215) 922-0796

Frank S. Schwarz & Son
1806 Chestnut Street
Philadelphia, PA 19103
(215) 563-4887

Anthony Stuempfig Antiques
2213 St. James Street
Philadelphia, PA 19103
(215) 561-7191

Theron Ware, Antiquarian
1600 Pine Street
Philadelphia, PA 19103
(215) 545-8492

Elinor Gordon
P.O. Box 211
Villanova, PA 19085
(215) 525-0981
   By appointment.

Chalfant & Chalfant
1352 Paoli Pike
West Chester, PA 19380
(215) 696-1862

C. L. Prickett Antiques
930 Stony Hill Road
Yardley, PA 19067
(215) 493-4284

Vermont

Brandon Antique Center
31 Franklin Street
Brandon, VT 05733
(802) 247-3026

Black Mountain Antique Center
Route 30
Brattleboro, VT 05301
(802) 254-3848

The Danby Antiques Center
Main Street
Danby, VT 05739
(802) 293-5484

Main Street Antiques Center
Danby Village, VT 05739
(802) 293-9919

Harold and DeDe Smith Antiques
Route 30, Box 509
Dorset, VT 05251
(802) 867-2271

The Antiques Center at Hartland
Route 5
Hartland, VT 05048
(802) 436-2441

Carriage Trade Antique Center
Route 7
Manchester, VT 05254
(802) 362-1125

1812 House Antique Center
RR 1, Box 2540
Manchester, VT 05255
(802) 362-1189

Nimmo & Hart Antiques
South Street, Rt. 133
Middletown Springs, VT 05757
(802) 235-2388

Peddler's Attic
Route 4
Quechee, VT 05059
(802) 296-2422

Factory Marketplace Antique Center
Route 22A
Vergennes, VT 05491
(802) 877-2975

Wallingford Antique Center
Main Street
Wallingford, VT 05773
(802) 446-2450

Woodstock Antiques Center
Route 4
Woodstock, VT 05091
(802) 457-4312

GREAT BRITAIN

London

Didier Aaron
21 Ryder Street
London SW1
(01) 839-4716

ADC Heritage
2 Old Bond Street
London W1
(01) 493-5088

Thomas Agnew & Sons
43 Old Bond Street
London W1
(01) 629-6176

Alfie's Antique Market
13-25 Church Street
London NW8
(01) 723-6066

Armin B. Allen
3 Bury Street
London SW1
(01) 930-4732

John Allsopp
26 Pimlico Road
London SW1
(01) 730-9347

Antigone Box Shop
Camden Passage
London N1
(01) 254-7074

Antiquarius
135-141 Kings Road
London SW3
(01) 351-5353

The Antique Porcelain Company
149 New Bond Street
London W1
(01) 629-1254

The Antique Textile Company
100 Portland Road
London W11
(01) 221-7730

Arenski
29-31 George Street
London W1
(01) 486-0678

Armitage
4 Davies Street
London W1
(01) 408-0675

Asprey & Company
165-169 New Bond Street
London W1
(01) 493-6767

Maurice Asprey
41 Duke Street
London SW1
(01) 930-3921

Louise Bannister
18 The Mall
Camden Passage
London N1
(01) 226-6665

Brian Beet
3B Burlington Gardens
London W1
(01) 437-4975

Raymond Benardout
4/5 William Street
London SW1
(01) 235-3360

Benardout & Benardout
7 Thurloe Place
London SW7
(01) 584-7658

Bennison
91 Pimlico Road
London SW1
(01) 730-8076

Charles Beresford-Clark
558 Kings Road
London SW6
(01) 731-5079

David Black Carpets
96 Portland Road
London W11
(01) 727-2566

Bluett & Sons
48 Davies Street
London W1
(01) 629-4018

Bond Street Antique Centre
124 New Bond Street
London W1
(01) 351-5353

Joanna Booth
247 Kings Road
London SW3
(01) 352-8998

J. H. Bourdon-Smith
24 Masons Yard
London SW1
(01) 839-4714

Nina Campbell
9 Walton Street
London SW3
(01) 225-1011

Caroline Carrier
Pierrepont Arcade
Camden Passage
London N1

Jack Casimir
23 Pembridge Road
London W11
(01) 727-8643

Chelsea Antique Market
245/253 Kings Road
London SW3
(01) 352-5689

Chelsea Clocks
479 Fulham Road
London SW6
(01) 731-5704

Chenil Galleries
181-183 Kings Road
London SW3
(01) 351-2077

Ciancimino Fine Art
99 Pimlico Road
London SW1
(01) 730-9950

Gerald Clark Antiques
1 High Street
London NW7
(01) 906-0342

Clifton Little Venice
3 Warwick Place
London W9
(01) 289-7894

Colefax and Fowler
39 Brook Street
London W1
(01) 493-2231

Philip Colleck
84 Fulham Road
London SW3
(01) 584-8479

Colnaghi
14 Old Bond Street
London W1
(01) 491-7408

Belinda Coote
29 Holland Street
London W8
(01) 937-3924

John Creed Antiques
Camden Passage
London N1
(01) 226-8867

T. Crowther & Son
282 North End Road
London SW6
(01) 385-1375

Arthur Davidson
78-79 Jermyn Street
London SW1
(01) 930-4643

Delomosne & Son
4 Campden Hill Road
London W8
(01) 937-1804

The Dining Room Shop
64 White Hart Lane
London SW13
(01) 878-1020

Donohoe
1-7 Davies Mews
London W1
(01) 629-5633

Eskenazi
166 Piccadilly
London W1
(01) 493-5464

Five Five Six Antiques
556 Kings Road
London SW6
(01) 731-2016

Kate Foster
9 Halkin Arcade
London SW1
(01) 245-9848

S. Frances
82 Jermyn Street
London SW1
(01) 235-1888

I. Freeman & Son
18 Dover Street
London W1
(01) 493-7658

Frognal Rare Books
18 Cecil Court
London WC2
(01) 240-2815

**Gallery of Antique Costume
and Textile**
2 Church Street
London NW8
(01) 723-9981

Garrard & Company
112 Regent Street
London W1
(01) 734-7020

G. Glass & Son
111/112 New Bond Street
London W1
(01) 493-5176

Thomas Goode & Company
19 South Audley Street
London W1
(01) 499-2823

Graham & Oxley
27 Bury Street
London SW1
(01) 229-1850

Gray's in Davies Mews
1-7 Davies Mews
and
Gray's in Davies Street
58 Davies Street
London W1
(01) 629-7034

Guinevere Antiques
578 Kings Road
London SW6
(01) 736-2917

Linda Gumb
19 The Mall
Camden Passage
London N1
(01) 354-1184

Gwyneth Antiques
56 Ebury Street
London SW1
(01) 730-2513

Halcyon Days
14 Brook Street
London W1
(01) 629-8811

Ross Hamilton
73 Pimlico Road
London SW1
(01) 730-3015

Rod Hanreck Antiques
11 Church Street
London NW8
(01) 724-9270

Harris Ltd.
6/8 Old Bond Street
London W1
(01) 499-0352

Jonathan Harris
54 Kensington Church Street
London W8
(01) 937-3133

Nicholas Harris
26 Conduit Street
London W1
(01) 499-5991

Jeanette Hayhurst
32a Kensington Church Street
London W8
(01) 938-1538

Heirloom & Howard
1 Hay Hill
London W1
(01) 493-5868

Linda Helm
117 Richmond Avenue
London N1
(01) 609-2716

Thomas Heneage & Co.
42 Duke Street
London SW1
(01) 930-9223

Hennell
12 New Bond Street
London W1
(01) 629-6888

Heraz
25 Motcomb Street
London SW1
(01) 245-9497

Hermitage
97 Pimlico Road
London SW1
(01) 730-1973

Hodsoll
50/69 Pimlico Road
London SW1
(01) 730-9835

Holland & Holland
33 Bruton Street
London W1
(01) 499-4411

Stephanie Hoppen
17 Walton Street
London SW3
(01) 589-3678

Jonathan Horne
66b/66c Kensington Church
Street
London W8
(01) 221-5658

Brand Inglis
9 Halkin Arcade
London SW1
(01) 235-6604

J & B Antiques
1A Kensington Church Walk
London W8
(01) 937-2335

Anthony James & Son
88 Fulham Road
London SW3
(01) 584-1120

Paul Jones
183 Kings Road
London SW3
(01) 351-2005

Jilly Kelly Antiques
19 Cambridge Street
London SW1
(01) 834-9703

David Ker Fine Art
85 Bourne Street
London SW1
(01) 730-8365

Klaber & Klaber
2A Bedford Gardens
London W8
(01) 727-4573

E. and C. T. Koopman & Son
The London Silver Vaults
Chancery House
Chancery Lane
London WC2
(01) 242-7624

The Lacquer Chest
75 Kensington Church Street
London W8
(01) 937-1306

Fiona and Bill Laidlaw
40 Gordon Place
London W8
(01) 937-8493

John, Jesse, & Irina Laski
160 Kensington Church Street
London W8
(01) 229-0312

Ronald A. Lee
1-9 Bruton Place
London W1
(01) 629-5600

M. P. Levine
5 Thurloe Place
London SW7
(01) 589-3755

Libra Antiques
131e Kensington Church Street
London W8
(01) 727-2990

Lindsay Antiques
99 Kensington Church Street
London W8
(01) 727-2333

Stephen Long Antiques
348 Fulham Road
London SW10
(01) 352-8226

Lunn Antiques
86 New Kings Road
London SW6
(01) 736-4638

The Mall Antiques Arcade
Camden Passage
London N1
(01) 354-2839

Magus
4 Church Street
London NW8
(01) 724-1278

Mallett & Son
40 New Bond Street
London W1
(01) 499-7411

D. M. & P. Manheim
69 Upper Berkeley Street
London W1

Mansfield
30-35 Drury Lane
London WC2
(01) 240-7780

The Map House of London
54 Beauchamp Place
London SW3
(01) 589-4325

S. Marchant & Son
120 Kensington Church Street
London W8
(01) 229-5319

Marlborough Rare Books
35 Old Bond Street
London W1
(01) 493-6993

David Martin-Taylor Antiques
56 Fulham High Street
London SW6
(01) 731-4135

Mayorcas
38 Jermyn Street
London SW1
(01) 629-4195

I. J. Mazure & Company
The London Silver Vaults
Vault No. 9
53 Chancery Lane
London WC2
(01) 242-3470

John Mitchell & Son
8 New Bond Street
London W1
(01) 493-7567

Mrs. Monro
11 Montpelier Street
London SW7
(01) 589-5052

H. W. Newby
15 Walton Street
London SW3
(01) 589-2752

Number Fifty-Six
56 Ebury Street
London SW1
(01) 730-2513

Raymond O'Shea Gallery
89 Lower Sloane Street
London SW1
(01) 730-0081

Partridge Fine Art
144-6 New Bond Street
London W1
(01) 629-0834

M. Pauw Antiques
561 Kings Road
London SW6
(01) 731-4022

Peel Antiques
131d Kensington Church
Street
London W8
(01) 727-8298

H. Perovetz
50-52 Chancery Lane
London WC2
(01) 405-8868

David Pettifer
269 Kings Road
London SW3
(01) 352-3088

S. J. Phillips
139 New Bond Street
London W1
(01) 629-6261

Portwine Galleries
175 Portobello Road
London W11
(01) 229-5305

Jonathan Potter
1 Grafton Street
London W1
(01) 491-3520

The Print Room
37 Museum Street
London WC1
(01) 430-0159

Pryce & Brise Antiques
79 Moore Park Road
London SW6
(01) 736-1864

Robert Pugh
31 Holland Street
London W8
(01) 937-6282

Punch Antiques
12 & 31 Georgian Village
Camden Passage
London N1
(01) 359-5863

Putnam's
Matthew's Yard
29 Shorts Gardens
London WC2
(01) 431-2935

Raffles Antiques
40 Church Street
London NW8
(01) 724-6384

Rede Hall Antiques
8 Pierrepont Arcade
Camden Passage
London N1

Rogers de Rin
76 Royal Hospital Road
London SW3
(01) 352-9007

Frank T. Sabin
3 Old Bond Street
London W1
(01) 499-5553

St. George's Gallery Books
8 Duke Street
London SW1
(01) 930-0935

St. Jude's Antiques
107 Kensington Church
Street
London W8
(01) 727-8737

Gerald Sattin
25 Burlington Arcade
London W1
(01) 493-6557

Charles Saunders
255 Fulham Road
London SW3
(01) 243-1828

Arthur Seager Antiques
25a Holland Street
London W8
(01) 937-3262

M. & D. Seligmann
37 Kensington Church
Street
London W8
(01) 727-3122

Jean Sewell
3 & 4 Campden Street
London W8
(01)) 727-3122

David Seyfreid
759 Fulham Road
London SW6
(01) 731-4230

Christine Schell
15 Cale Street
London SW3
(01) 352-5563

S. J. Shrubsole
43 Museum Street
London WC1
(01) 405-2712

Keith Skeel
94 Islington High Street
London N1
(01) 226-7012

Colin Smith & Gerald Robinson Antiques
105 Portobello Road
London W11
(01) 994-3783

Peta Smyth
42 Moreton Street
London SW1
(01) 630-9898

Henry Sotheran
2-5 Sackville Street
London W1
(01) 734-1150

Spink & Son
5-7 King Street
London SW1
(01) 930-7888

Stair & Company
120 Mount Street
London W1
(01) 499-1784

Serena Stapleton Antiques
75 Lower Richmond Road
London SW15
(01) 789-4245

Constance Stobo
31 Holland Street
London W8
(01) 937-6282

Carolyn Stoddart-Scott
London W8
(01) 727-5045
    By appointment.

Richard Stokes Antiques
104 Kensington Church Street
London W8
(01) 727-0548

Mr. F. Storey-Mendler
293 Westbourne Grove
London W11
(01) 452-6193

Tessiers
26 New Bond Street
London W1
(01) 629-0458

Pamela Teignmouth & Sons
108 Kensington Church Street
London W8
(01) 229-1602

S. & A. Thompson
135 Kings Road
London SW3
(01) 352-3494

Jan Van Beers
1-7 Davies Mews
London W1
(01) 408-0434

Earle D. Vandekar of Knightsbridge
138 Brompton Road
London SW3
(01) 589-8481

Valerie Wade
89 Ebury Street
London SW1
(01) 730-3822

Wartski
14 Grafton Street
London W1
(01) 493-1141

J. V. Webb
12 Pierrepont Row
Camden Passage
London N1
(01) 359-2641

Wenderton Antiques
26 Cornwallis Road
London N19
(01) 263-2786

Arnold Wiggins & Sons
30-34 Woodfield Place
London W9
(01) 286-9656

O. F. Wilson
Queen's Elm Parade
London SW3
(01) 352-9554

Mary Wise
27 Holland Street
London W8
(01) 937-8649

Joanna Wood
48a Pimlico Road
London SW1
(01) 730-5064

York Arcade
Camden Passage
London N1
(01) 837-8768

Robert Young Antiques
68 Battersea Bridge Road
London SW11
(01) 228-7847

Provincial

**William Young (Aberdeen)
Ltd**
1 Belmont Street
Aberdeen AB1 1JR
(0224) 644757

S. and S. Timms Antiques Ltd
16-20 Dunstable Street
Ampthill
Bedfordshire
(0525) 403067

Michael Webb Fine Art
Cefn-Llwyn, Llangristiolus
Bodorgan
Anglesey
(0407) 840336

Trevor Micklem Antiques Ltd
Withywine Farm
Morebath
Bampton
Devon EX16 9BZ
(0398) 31409

Andrew Dando
4 Wood Street
Queen Square
Bath
Avon BA1 2JQ
(0225) 22702

D. and B. Dickinson
The Antique Shop
22 and 22a New Bond Street
Bath
Avon BA1 1BA
(0225) 66502

Richard Parker Ltd
Trim Bridge
1 Queen Street
Bath
Avon BA1 1HE
(0225) 330257

Park Street Antiques
350 High Street
Berkhamstead
Hertfordshire HP4 1HT
(044 27) 4790

E. M. Cheshire
The Manor House
Market Place
Bingham
Nottinghamshire NG13 8AP
(0949) 38861

Pamela Rowan
High Street
Blockley
Gloucestershire GL56 9ET
(0386) 700280

Avon Antiques
26-27 Market Street
Bradford-on-Avon
Wiltshire DA15 1LL
(022 16) 2052

Michael Norman Antiques Ltd
15 Ship Street
Brighton
East Sussex BN1 1AD
(0273) 29253/4

Robin N. H. Butler
20 Clifton Road
Bristol
Avon BS8 1AQ
(0272) 733017

H. W. Keil Ltd
Tudor House
Broadway
Hereford and Worcester
WR12 7DP
(0386) 852408

Zene Walker
The Bull House
High Street
Burford
Oxfordshire OX8 4RH
(099 382) 3284

John Beazor and Sons Ltd
78-80 Regent Street
Cambridge CB2 1DP
(0223) 355178

Combe Cottage Antiques
Castle Combe
Nr Chippenham
Wiltshire SN14 7HU
(0249) 782250

H. W. Keil Ltd
129-131 The Promenade
Cheltenham
Gloucestershire GL50 1NW
(0242) 522509

Adams Antiques
65 Watergate Row
Chester
(0244) 319421

William H. Stokes
Roberts House
Siddington
Nr Cirencester
Gloucestershire GL7 6EX
(0285) 67101

Partner and Puxon
7 and 16 North Hill
Colchester
Essex CO1 1DZ
(0206) 573317

Patrick Worth Antiques
11 West Street
Dorking
Surrey RH4 1BL
(0306) 884484

William Bruford & Son Ltd
11 and 13 Cornfield Road
Eastbourne
East Sussex BN21 3NA
(0323) 25452

David Letham
23 Gloucester Lane
Edinburgh EH3 6ED
(031) 225-7399

Windsor Antiques
80 High Street
Eton
Berkshire
(0753) 860752

William Bruford & Son Ltd
1 Bedford Street
Exeter
Devon EX1 1LU
(0392) 54901

A. and F. Partners
20 London Street
Faringdon
Oxfordshire SN7 7AA
(0367) 20078

**Barclay Lennie Fine
Art Ltd**
203 Bath Street
Glasgow
(041) 226-5413

Heath-Bullock
8 Meadrow
Godalming
Surrey GU7 3HN
(048 68) 22562

G. Oliver and Sons
St Catherine's House
Portsmouth Road
Guildford
Surrey GU3 1LJ
(0483) 575427

**W. F. Greenwood &
Sons Ltd**
2 and 3 Crown Place
Harrogate
North Yorkshire HG1 2RY
(0423) 504467

Peter Foyle Hunwick
The Old Malthouse
15 Bridge Street
Hungerford
Berkshire RG17 0EG
(0488) 82209

Stephen Moore Ltd
103 High Street
Lewes
East Sussex BN7 1XH
(0273) 474158

David J. Hansord (Antiques)
32 Steep Hill
Lincoln LN2 1LU
(0522) 30044

Maureen Thompson
The Sun House
Hall Street
Long Melford
Suffolk CO10 9HZ
(0787) 78252

Kenworthy's Ltd
226 Stamford Street
Ashton-under-Lyne
Manchester OL6 7LW
(061) 330-3043

Nigel Craknell (Antiques) Ltd
Cavendish House
138 High Street
Marlborough
Wiltshire SN8 1HN
(0672) 52912

Michael Toone
Tudors
Church Hill
Midhurst
West Sussex GU29 9NX
(073 081) 2519

Simon Brett
Creswyke House
High Street
Moreton-in-Marsh
Gloucestershire GL56 0LH
(0608) 50751

John Barry
Barton End Hall
Nr Nailsworth
Gloucestershire GL6 0QQ
(045 383) 3471

New Abbey Antiques
Caragh Lodge
Glen Road
Newtownabbey
Co Antrim BT37 0RY
Northern Ireland
(0231) 62036

**Arthur Brett and
Sons Ltd**
42 St Giles Street
Norwich
Norfolk NR2 1LW
(0603) 628171

The Antiquary
50 St Giles
Oxford OX1 3LU
(0865) 59875

Northgate Antiques
10 Northgate Street
Pembroke
(0646) 684416

Walter S. Beaton
75 Kinnoull Street
Perth PH1 5EZ
(0738) 28127

Richard Davidson Antiques
Lombard Street
Petworth
West Sussex GU28 0AG
(0798) 42508

Donald Allison Antiques
115-119 New Hall Lane
Preston
Lancashire
(0772) 701916

Lewis & Lloyd
13 West Street
Reigate
Surrey RH2 9BL

**Millers of Chelsea
Antiques Ltd**
Netherbrook House
86 Christchurch Road
Ringwood
Hampshire
(04254) 2062

Ian G. Hastie
46 St Ann Street
Salisbury
Wiltshire SP1 2DX
(0722) 22957

G. W. Ford & Son Ltd
290 Glossop Road
Sheffield
South Yorkshire S10 2HS
(0742) 22082

Douglas Gordon Antiques
The Old Rectory
Stockbridge
Hampshire SO20 6EU
(0264) 810662

Christopher Clarke
The Fosse Way
Stow-on-the-Wold
Gloucestershire GL54 1JS
(0451) 30476

Simon W. Nutter
Wraggs Row
Fosse Way
Stow-on-the-Wold
Gloucestershire GL54 1GT
(0451) 30658

Arbour Antiques Ltd
Poet's Arbour
Sheep Street
Stratford-upon-Avon
Warwickshire CV37 6EF
(0789) 293453

Thomas Coulborn & Sons
Vesey Manor
64 Birmingham Road
Sutton Coldfield
West Midlands B72 1QP
(021) 354-3974

George S. Bolam
Oak House
1 The Chipping
Tetbury
Gloucestershire GL8 8EU
(0666) 52211

Turpin's Antiques
4 Stoney Lane
Thaxted
Essex CM6 2PF
(0371) 830495

Derek Roberts Antiques
24 Shipbourne Road
Tonbridge
Kent TN10 3DN
(0732) 358986

John Bly
50 High Street
Tring
Hertfordshire HP23 5AG
(044 282) 3030

**Leonard Lassalle (Antiques)
Limited**
21 The Pantiles
Tunbridge Wells
Kent TN2 5TD
(0892) 31645

Summers Davis & Sons Ltd
Calleva House
High Street
Wallingford
Oxfordshire OX10 0BP
(0491) 36284

Edward Nowell & Sons
21-23 Market Place
Wells
Somerset BA5 2RF
(0749) 72415

Paul Hopwell Antiques Ltd
30 High Street
West Haddon
Northamptonshire NN6 7AP
(078 887) 636

R. Saunders
71 Queen's Road
Weybridge
Surrey KT13 9UQ
(0932) 42601

J. W. Blanchard
12 Jewry Street
Winchester
Hampshire SO23 8RZ
(0962) 54547

Guy Bousfield
58 Thames Street
Windsor
Berkshire SL4 1QW
(0753) 864575

**Anthony Scaramanga
Antiques**
108 Newland
Witney
Oxfordshire OX8 6JN
(0993) 3472

Christopher Sykes Antiques
The Old Parsonage
Woburn
Bedfordshire MK17 9QL
(0525) 25259

David Gibbins Antiques
21 Market Hill
Woodbridge
Suffolk 1P12 4LX
(039 43) 3531

Robert Morrison & Son
Trentholme House
131 The Mount
York YO2 2DA
(0904) 55394

AUSTRALIA

Sydney

Brian Moore and John Paradee
42 Queen Street
Woollahra NSW 2025
(02) 32 0521

Martyn Cook Antiques
104 Queen Street
Woollahra NSW 2025
(02) 328 1801/2

W. F. Bradshaw
(clocks, keyboard instruments)
96 Queen Street
Woollahra NSW 2025
(02) 32 4453

Anne Schofield
(jewellery)
36 Queen Street
Woollahra NSW 2025
(02) 32 1326

Coddington Antiques
742 Military Road
Mosman NSW 2088
(02) 960 3427

J. B. Hawkins
7 Amherst
Cammeray NSW 2062
(02) 92 4692

Robert Morrison
84 Queen Street
Woollahra NSW 2025
(02) 323 273

Melbourne

A complimentary guide booklet is available. Contact: John Furphy, Acorn Antiques (03) 509 8602 or Henry Greener, Phoenix Antiques (03) 51 9607.

John D. Dunn
1431 Malvern Road
Malvern 3144
(03) 205 637

Kozminsky's
421 Bourke Street
Melbourne
(03) 670 1277

Lee Harper
1009 High Street
Armadale VIC 3143
(03) 205 943

Grace Antique Galleries
1120 High Street
Armadale VIC 3143
(03) 509 8680

South Australia

Cavalier Antiques
602 Brighton Road
Seacliff SA 5049
(08) 296 5126

H. G. Quigley Antiques
427 Pulteney Street
Adelaide SA
(08) 223 7794

Western Australia

Stirling Galleries
163 Stirling Highway
Nedlands WA
(09) 386 5161

Goodwood House Antiques
84-86 Goodwood Parade
Rivervale WA 6103
(09) 361 6368

Queensland

Cintra Galleries
40 Bark Street
Milton
Brisbane QLD
(07) 369 1322

Douglas Antiques
96 Margaret Street
Toowoomba QLD
(076) 32 7148

Toowoomba Gallery
100 Margaret Street
Toowoomba QLD
(076) 385 355

Warlock Antiques
33 Logan Road
Woolloongabba QLD 4102
(07) 391 6919

Hinds Antiques
34 Florence Street
Tenerife QLD 4005

Tasmania

De Witt Antiques
52 Bathurst Street
Battery Point
Hobart TAS 7000
(002) 234 998

Roberts Antiques
6 Collins Street
Hobart TAS
(002) 234 200

Longford Antiques
38 Marlborough Street
Longford TAS
(003) 911 571

Windsor Antiques
271-273 Hobart Road
Kings Meadows
Launceston TAS
(003) 449 971

NEW ZEALAND

Richard Matthews Antiques
Remuera, Auckland
(09) 540 310

Portobello Antiques
Parnell, Auckland
(09) 732 013

David Cooke
Shortland Street
Auckland
(09) 734 325

Donald Melville Antiques
Takapuna, Auckland
(09) 496 513

John Dixon's Antiques
Remuera, Auckland
(09) 502 603

Barry Thomas Antiques
Remuera, Auckland
(09) 504 090

William & Mary
Victoria Street
Hamilton
(071) 395 305

Colonial Heritage
Duke Street
Cambridge
(071) 274 211

Catherine Hannah Antiques
Haupapa Street
Rotorua
(073) 86 617

Philip Rhodes Antiques
North Street
Palmerston North
(063) 78 487

Elizabeth Wilkin Antiques
BNZ Centre, Wellington
(04) 736 804

Marsden Antiques
Brooklyn, Wellington
(04) 850 152

Antique Imports
Lower Hutt, Wellington
(04) 697 019

Brentwood Antiques
Walterwoods
Matahiwi Road
Masterton
(089) 84 385

W. Holliday & Sons Ltd.
Papanui Road
Merivale, Christchurch
(03) 554 117

Vaughan Antiques
Victoria Street
Christchurch
(03) 798 521

Hopkinson's Antiques Ltd.
Hilton Highway
Timaru
(056) 82 772

FRANCE
Paris

Didier Aaron & Cie
118 Faubourg Saint-Honoré
Paris, France 75008
(01) 47-42-47-34

Antiquités 54
54 rue Jacob
Paris, France 75006
(01) 42-60-83-61

Au Bain Marie
10 rue Boissy d'Anglos
Paris, France 75008
(01) 42-66-59-74

Aux Fils du Temps
33 rue de Grenelle
Paris, France 75007
(01) 45-48-14-68

Aux "Impressions du Passe"
41 rue de Verneuil
Paris, France 75007
(01) 42-61-37-29

Georges Bac
35-37 rue Bonaparte
Paris, France 75006
(01) 43-26-82-67

Dario Boccara
184 rue du Faubourg Saint-Honoré
Paris, France 75008
(01) 43-59-84-63

Bousquet et Cie
57 rue du Cherche Midi
Paris, France 75006
(01) 45-48-33-50

Galerie Camoin
9 Quai Voltaire
Paris, France 75007
(01) 42-61-82-06

Anne Caracciolo
16 rue de l'Université
Paris, France 75007
(01) 42-61-22-22

Madeleine Castaing
21 rue Bonaparte
Paris, France 75006
(01) 43-54-91-71

Lucienne Cella
Place des Vosges
2 rue des Francs-Bourgeois
Paris, France 75003
(01) 42-77-40-53

Charette
22 rue Jean Giraudoux
Paris, France 75006
(01) 47-20-11-79

Galerie Chevalier
15 Quai Voltaire
Paris, France 75007
(01) 42-60-72-68

Galerie Coligny
138 rue Saint-Honoré
Paris, France 75001
(01) 42-60-21-51

La Cour aux Antiquaires
54 rue de Faubourg Saint-Honoré
Paris, France 75008
(01) 47-42-43-99

Jean Pierre DeCastro
17 rue des Francs Bourgeois
Paris, France 75003
(01) 42-72-04-00

Claude De Clerq
15 rue Étienne
Paris, France 75001
(01) 42-36-30-01

Edrei
44 rue de Lille
Paris, France 75007
(01) 42-61-28-08

Godard-Desmarest
178 rue du Faubourg Saint-Honoré
Paris, France 75008
(01) 45-63-71-01

Jardin d'Ispahan
9 rue de Bassano
Paris, France 75016
(01) 47-20-38-95

Kugel
279 rue Saint-Honoré
Paris, France 75008
(01) 42-60-86-23

LeFebvre et Fils
24 rue de Bac
Paris, France 75007
(01) 42-61-16-40

Le Louvre des Antiquaires
2 Place du Palais Royal
Paris, France 75001
(01) 42-97-27-00

Maison Josephine
1 rue Bonaparte
Paris, France 75006
(01) 43-26-49-73

Meunier Batifaud
38 Boulevard Raspail
Paris, France 75007
(01) 45-48-05-78

Michel Meyer
24 Avenue Matignon
Paris, France 75008
(01) 42-66-62-95

Nicole Mugler
2 rue de l'Université
Paris, France 75007
(01) 42-96-36-45

Niclausse
50 rue la Bruyère
Paris, France 75009
(01) 48-74-11-49

Nicolier
7 Quai Voltaire
Paris, France 75007
(01) 42-60-78-63

Michel Ottin
33 Quai Voltaire
Paris, France 75007
(01) 42-61-19-88

Librairie Pinault
36 rue Bonaparte
Paris, France 75006
(01) 46-33-04-24

Mme. Polles
131 Faubourg Saint-Honoré
Paris, France 75008
(01) 42-25-05-39

Bernard Steinitz
4 rue Drouot
Paris, France 75009
(01) 42-46-98-98

Village St. Paul
Rue St. Paul
Paris, France 75005

Village Suisse
L'Avenue Motte Picquet
Paris, France 75015

ITALY
Florence

Alberghini Antichita
22/R Via Maggio
Florence, Italy 50123
(055) 214-569

Guido Bartolozzi
18/R Via Maggio
Florence, Italy 50123
(055) 215-602

Luca Battaglini
76/R Borgo San Jacopo
Florence, Italy 50125
(055) 262-206

Luigi Bellini e Figli
5 Lungarno Soderini
Florence, Italy 50124
(055) 214-031

Carlo Carnevali
64R Borgo San Jacopo
Florence, Italy 50125
(055) 295-064

Carlo De Carlo
16 Via di Camerata
Florence, Italy 50133
(055) 587-011

Antichita Roberto di Clemente
64R Via Maggio
Florence, Italy 50123
(055) 296-649

Falteri
40/R Via Benci
Florence, Italy 50122
(055) 243-704

Michele and Catherine Finck
15/R Via della Vigni Muova
Florence, Italy 50125
(055) 213-243

Enrico Frascione
61/R Via dei Fossi
Florence, Italy 50123
(055) 294-087

Galleria San Jacopo
49/R Borgo San Jacopo
Florence, Italy 50125
(055) 210-334

Fioretto Giampaolo
43/R Borgo Ognissanti
Florence, Italy 50123
(055) 214-927

Antichita Gianfrance Luzzetti
28/A Borgo San Jacopo
Florence, Italy 50125
(055) 211-232

Mary Pavan de Carlo
1/R Via Maggio
Florence, Italy 50123
(055) 298-029

Alberto Pierini
22/R Borgo Ognissanti
Florence, Italy 50123
(055) 298-138

Mirella Piselli
23/R Via Maggio
Florence, Italy 50123
(055) 298-029

Paolo Romano
20/R Borgo Ognissanti
Florence, Italy 50123
(055) 293-294

Antichita Santoro
8/R Via Mazzetta
Florence, Italy 50125
(055) 213-116

Lo Spillo
76/R Borgo San Jacopo
Florence, Italy 50125
(055) 293-196

Pasquale Velona
31/R Via dei Fossi
Florence, Italy 50100
(055) 587-069

Paola Ventura
16-17/R Borgo Ognissanti
Florence, Italy 50123
(055) 210-914

Milan

Arte Antica
11 Via San Andrea
Milan, Italy 20121
(02) 791-776

Tino Bellini
4 Via San Carpoforo
Milan, Italy 20121
(02) 872-963

Antichita Bonatelli
25/A Via Niccolini
Milan, Italy 20154
(02) 331-1957

Paolo Canelli
14 Via Santo Spirito
Milan, Italy 20121
(02) 702-124

Amadeo Cocchi
5 Via Rossari
Milan, Italy 20121
(02) 701-837

D'A Tea
2 Via Maggiolini
Milan, Italy 20122
(02) 791-256

Roberto Dabbene
1 Largo Treves
Milan, Italy 20121
(02) 655-4406

Dario Ghio
30 C. 50 Magenta
Milan, Italy 20123
(02) 862-324

La Grange Antichita
63 Viale Montenero
Milan, Italy 20121
(02) 545-8656

Davide Halevim
13 Via Santo Spirito
Milan, Italy 20121
(02) 702-292

A. Subert Jarach
2 Largo Bellintani
Milan, Italy 20124
(02) 204-6677

Nella Longari
15 Via Bigli
Milan, Italy 20121
(02) 794-287

Nilufar
4 Via Bigli
Milan, Italy 20121
(02) 780-193

Ornamenti D'Epoca
21 Via Ponte Vetero
Milan, Italy 20121
(02) 688-7509

Antichita Pelgoron
16 Corso Europa
Milan, Italy 20122
(02) 701-591

Bomenico Piva
1 Via Sant'Andrea
Milan, Italy 20121
(02) 700-698

Le Quinte di Via dell-Orso
14 Via dell'Orso
Milan, Italy 20121

Franco Sabatelli
5 Via Fiori Chiari
Milan, Italy 20121

Florence Taccani
24 Via Santo Spirito
Milan, Italy 20121
(02) 781-248

Carlo Teardo
2 Via Maggiolini
Milan, Italy 20122
(02) 791-356

ANTIQUES MARKETS
AND CENTRES

Browsing in outdoor antiques markets has become a very popular pastime. In Europe there is an outdoor market almost every day of the week. Some have been there since the turn of the century, and they are open all year round.

GREAT BRITAIN

Antiques markets exist in towns and cities throughout Britain. Here are some of the best known.

Bath Antiques Market
Guinea Lane
Lansdown Road
Bath
Avon
Open Wednesday, 6:30 A.M. to 2:30 P.M. The market offers both dealers and the public, who travel from all over the country to buy and sell, some of the best pieces and prices to be found anywhere.

Bermondsey (New Caledonian) Market
Bermondsey Street and Long Lance
London SE1

Open Fridays, 5 A.M. to 1 P.M. Getting here could be a problem, so take a taxi. Dress warmly in early morning and in winter, since most of the market is outside, and take a flashlight. Several acres covered with long aisles of stalls are filled with antiques supposedly found that week in the countryside.

Camden Passage
Islington
London N1
Open Wednesday, 7:30 A.M. to 2 P.M.; Saturday, 10 A.M. to 2 P.M. I prefer going to Camden Passage on Wednesdays when there are more outdoor stalls filling every inch between the indoor markets, shops, and arcades. Start at The Mall and don't stop until you get to the Georgian Village at the other end.

Church Street Market
Marylebone
London NW8
Open Tuesday to Saturday, 9 A.M. to 5 P.M. I usually go to this market on Tuesday. It consists of outdoor stalls along Church Street. Be sure to visit Alfie's Antiques Market, which has

200 dealers, and other nearby shops when you are at the Church Street Market.

Jubilee Market
Covent Garden
London WC2
Open Monday, 7 A.M. to 2 P.M. A relatively new market with 200 stalls on the site of the old Covent Garden Piazza, it has some crafts and small antiques.

Portobello Road Market
Portobello Road
London W10
Open Saturday, 9 A.M. to 5 P.M. A long road lined with arcades, stalls, vans, and barrows filled to the brim with every kind of antique imaginable. Start at the top and walk down. If you have time, look in the shops in Westbourne Grove, which bisects Portobello.

Many towns also have antiques centres or arcades, which bring together a number of dealers under one roof, and which are usually open every day. Here are a few examples.

Woburn Abbey Antiques Centre
Woburn, Bedfordshire
Open daily, 11 A.M. to 5 P.M.
including Sundays and Bank Holidays.

Cheltenham Antique Market
54 Suffolk Road
Cheltenham, Gloucestershire
Open Monday to Saturday, 9:30 A.M.
to 5:30 P.M.

Oxford Antiques Centre
The Jam Factory
27 Park End Street
Oxford
Open Tuesday to Saturday, 10 A.M.
to 5 P.M. and first Sunday in month
11 A.M. to 5 P.M.

Antiquarius
131-141 King's Road
London SW3
Open Monday to Saturday, 10 A.M. to
6 P.M.

Chenil Galleries
181-183 King's Road
London SW3
Open Monday to Saturday, 10 A.M. to
6 P.M.

Bond Street Antiques Centre
124 New Bond Street
London W1
Open Monday to Saturday, 10 A.M. to
5:45 P.M.

AUSTRALIA

Mosman Portobello
742 Military Road
Mosman NSW 2088
(02) 960 3427

Sydney Antique Centre
531 South Dowling Street
Surry Hills NSW 2010
(02) 333 244

The Woollahra Galleries
160 Oxford Street
Woollahra NSW 2025
(02) 327 8840

Maling Road Antique Market
117 Maling Road
Canterbury VIC
(03) 836 8927

The Melbourne Antique Centre
941 High Street
Armadale VIC 3143
(03) 822 7102

The Antique Centre
26 Leigh Street
Adelaide SA 5000
(08) 231 3071

WA Antique Centre
32 Northwood Street
West Leederville WA 6007
(09) 381 1957

Brisbane Antique Markets
791 Sandgate Road
Playfield QLD
(07) 262 1444

Paddington Antique Centre
167 Latrobe Terrace
Paddington QLD 4064
(07) 369 8458

Hobart Antique Centre
59 Salamanca Place
Hobart TAS 7000
(002) 240 040

FRANCE

Marché Aux Puces
Porte de Clignancourt
Saint-Ouen
Paris, France
Open Saturdays, Sundays, and Mondays, but I usually go on Saturday at
10:00 A.M. There are about 3,000

dealers in 10 separate markets
covering 75 acres, selling everything from used clothing to valuable
antiques. My favorite markets are
the Marchés Biron and Paul-Bert.

ITALY

Rome Flea Market
Porta Portese
Viale Trastevere
Rome, Italy 00153
Open Sunday, 6:30 A.M. to 1 P.M.
This immensely popular, colorful
weekly market has everything from
clothes to wonderful antiques.

ANTIQUES SHOWS AND FAIRS

Antiques shows always have a
special flavor and have merchandise that is varied and interesting. Many of them—for
example, Grosvenor House in
London—have become social
events looked forward to each
season. Show management details are included so you can call
or write for dates and locations.

GREAT BRITAIN

The Annual Welsh Antiques Fair
Information: Antiques in Britain Fairs
Brecon
Powys
(054 74) 356

The British International Antiques Fair
Information: N.E.C.
National Exhibition Centre
Birmingham
(021) 780-4141

The Burlington House Fair
Information: 6 Bloomsbury Square
London WC1
(01) 430-0481

The City of Bath Antiques Fair
Information: Robert Bailey
Pavilion Rooms
Bath
(01) 550-5435

The Chelsea Antiques Fair
Information: Penman Antiques Fairs
Caroline Penman
Lindfield, Haywards Heath
West Sussex RH16
(0447) 2514

The Decorative Antiques and Textiles Fair
Information: Harvey Management Services, Ltd.
P.O. Box 149
London W9
(01) 624-5173

East Anglia Antiques Fair
Information: Antiques in Britain Fairs
Bury St Edmunds
Suffolk
(054 74) 356

The Fine Art and Antiques Fair Olympia
Information: Philbeach Events Limited
Warwick Road
London SW5
(01) 385-1200

The Grosvenor House Antiques Fair
Information: Evan Steadman & Partners, Ltd.
The Hub, Emson Close
Saffron Walden CB10
(0799) 26699

The Harrogate Antiques Fair
Information: The Harrogate Antiques and Fine Art Fair Ltd.
The Crown Hotel
Harrogate
(0423) 67933

The International Ceramics Fair
Information: Brian and Anna Haughton
3B Burlington Gardens
London W1X
(01) 381-1324

The International Silver and Jewelry Fair
Information: 3B Burlington Gardens
Old Bond Street
London W1X
(01) 734-5491

The London Antique Dealers' Fair
Information: Jane Sunmer
Cafe Royal
Regent Street
London W1
(0799) 23611

Newton Abbot Giant Antique & Collectors Fair
Information: West Country Antiques and Collectors Fairs
Newton Abbot
Devon
(0364) 52182

Northern Ireland Antique Dealers' Fair
Information: Castle Fairs Ltd.
Holywood, Northern Ireland
(0937) 832029

Northern Antiques Fair
Information: Manor House
High Birstwith
Harrogate HG3
(0423) 770385

Park Lane Hotel Antiques Fair
Information: Guy Hutson Public Relations
10 Dukes Avenue
London W4
(01) 995-5094

The Scottish Antiques Fair
Information: Antiques in Britain Fairs
Edinburgh
(054 74) 356

The West and Wales Antique Ceramics Fairs
Information: Antiques in Britain Fairs
Chepstow
Gwent
(054 74) 356

The West of England Antiques Fair
Information: Anne Campbell-Macinnes
Bristol Exhibition Centre
(0225) 63727

West London Antiques Fair
Information: Penman Antiques Fairs
Kensington Town Hall
London W8
(04447) 2514

AUSTRALIA

Giant Syndey Antique Fair
Sydney Show Ground (June)
Largest in the Southern Hemisphere
Contact: Alan Carter
(02) 905 1588

Australian Antique Trader
162 Goulbun Street
Darlinghurst NSW 2010
(02) 816 4614

New South Wales Antique Dealers Associations Fair
Information: Executive Secretary
Mrs Joanne Minogue
(02) 331 5176
or President Mr Ian Fraser
(02) 660 3019
Vacluse House

Antique Dealers Association of Victoria Annual Fair
Information: G. Cook
P.O. Box 24
Malvern 3144

The Festival of Antiques
Sponsored by SA Antique Dealers Association
Information: President Peter Quigley
Megaw and Hogg Antiques Pty Ltd
26 Leigh Street
Adelaide SA
(08) 213 0101

Perth Antique Fair
Information: Alan Donnolly & Assoc.
(09) 388 2788
or Society of Crippled Children
(09) 384 1855
Clairmont Show Ground

Brisbane Antique Fair
Information: Nick Warlock
(07) 391 6919
Exhibition Building, R.N.A. Grounds
Gregory Terrace
Brisbane QLD

Tasmanian Antique Dealers Association Annual Fair
Information: Michael McWilliam
Longford Antiques
Marlborough Street
Longford TAS
(003) 911 571
Albert Hall, Launceston

Canberra Antique Fair
Organised by National Trust and NSW Antique Dealers Association
Information: Charles Aronson
Aronson Antiques
317 Pacific Highway
Crows Nest
(02) 922 3610
Albert Hall

**Antique Dealers Guild of
Australia Fair**
Information: David Cameron
Jupiters Antiques
173 Latrobe Terrace
Paddington QLD 4064
(07) 369 4433
Held in November in Brisbane

NEW ZEALAND

The New Zealand Antique
Dealers Association have annual
fairs in Auckland, Wellington,
Christchurch, and Dunedin. An
annual antiques fair, organised by
Rotary International, is held at
the Ellerslie racecourse every
June-July. A fair at the Chase
Stadium, Auckland, takes place at
the end of each year.

FRANCE

**Antique Dealers Fair in
Toulouse**
Information: Sforman, S.A.
31 rue du Rampart Matabiau
Toulouse, France 31000
(1) 61-21-93-25

**Biennale Internationale des
Antiquaires**
Information: 11 rue Jean-Mermoz
Paris, France 75008
(01) 42-25-44-33

**International Brocante &
Antiques Fair**
Information: Mme. Resse
18 rue Lénine
Ivry-sur-Seine, France 94200
(1) 46-71-66-14

ITALY

**Biennale Internazionale dell'
Antiquariato**
Palazzo Strozzi
Via Tournabuoni
Florence, Italy 50123
(055) 282-635

Internazionale dell'Antiquariato
Via Spinola
Milan, Italy 20122
Information: EXPO CT
Via Serbelloni, 2
Milan, Italy 20122
(02) 784-551

AUCTIONS

One of the best places to see the
decorative and fine arts and educate yourself about them is the
auction room. Attending auctions
will give you a feeling of what's
happening in the marketplace.
It's fun to look even if you're not
planning to buy.

UNITED STATES
Connecticut

Litchfield Auction Gallery
Route 202
Litchfield, CT 06759
(203) 567-4303

Winter Associates Inc.
21 Cook Street
Plainville, CT 06062
(203) 793-0288

District of Columbia

C. G. Sloan & Company
919 E Street N.W.
Washington, DC 20004
(202) 628-1468

Adam A. Weschler & Sons
905–9 E Street N.W.
Washington, DC 20004
(202) 628-1281

Massachusetts

Robert W. Skinner
2 Newbury Street
Boston, MA 02116
(617) 236-1700

Robert C. Eldred & Co.
Route 6A
East Dennis, MA 02641
(617) 385-3116

Richard A. Bourne Co., Inc.
P.O. Box 141
Hyannis, MA 02647
(617) 775-0797

New York

Christie's
502 Park Avenue
New York, NY 10022
(212) 546-1000

Christie's East
219 East 67 Street
New York, NY 10021
(212) 570-4141

William Doyle Galleries
175 East 87 Street
New York, NY 10028
(212) 427-2730

Guernsey's
136 East 73 Street
New York, NY 10021
(212) 794-2280

Phillips
406 East 79 Street
New York, NY 10021
(212) 570-4830

Sotheby's
1334 York Avenue
New York, NY 10021
(212) 606-7000

Swann Galleries
104 East 25 Street
New York, NY 10010
(212) 254-4710

GREAT BRITAIN

London

Bonham's
65-69 Lots Road
London SW10
(01) 351-7111

Bonham's Montpelier Galleries
Montpelier Street
Knightsbridge
London SW7 1HH
(01) 584-9161

Christie's
B. King Street
St. James
London SW1
(01) 839-9060

Christie's South Kensington
85 Old Brompton Road
London SW7
(01) 581-2231

Lots Road Galleries
71 Lots Road
London SW10
(01) 351-7771

Phillips
10 Salem Road
London W2
(01) 229-9090

Phillips Fine Art Auctioneers
7 Blenheim Street
New Bond Street
London W1
(01) 629-6602

Sotheby's
34/35 New Bond Street
London W1
(01) 493-8080

Provincial

Sotheby's, Christie's and Phillips
have representatives throughout
the United Kingdom and Ireland;
a list can be obtained from their
London offices. There are also
many independent auction houses
throughout the country which can
be found in the Yellow Pages.
Here are a few examples.

Anderson & Garland
Anderson House
Market Street
Newcastle-upon-Tyne NE1 6XA
(091) 232-6278

William H Brown Ltd
Stanilands Auction Room
28 Netherhall Road
Doncaster
South Yorkshire DN1 2PW
(0302) 67766

William H. Brown Ltd
Westgate Hall
Westgate
Grantham
Lincolnshire NG31 6LT
(0476) 68861

Bruton Knowles & Co.
Albion Chambers
55 Barton Street
Gloucester GL1 1PZ
(0452) 21267

H. C. Chapman & Son
The Auction Mart
North Street
Scarborough
North Yorkshire YO11 1DL
(0723) 372424

Henry Duke & Son
40 South Street
Dorchester
Dorset DT1 1DG
(0305) 65080

John Francis
Thomas Jones and Sons
19 King Street
Carmarthen
Dyfed SA31 1JR
(0267) 233456

**Lawrence Fine Art of
Crewkerne**
South Street
Crewkerne
Somerset TA18 8AB
(0460) 73041

Messenger, May & Baverstock
Sundial House
High Street
Godalming
Surrey GU6 8AE
(0483) 273891

**Michael Newman Fine Art
Auctioneers & Valuers**
The Central Auction Rooms
Kinterbury House
St Andrews Cross
Plymouth
Devon PL1 2DQ
(0752) 669298

Prudential Fine Art Auctioneers
Fine Art Auction Galleries
Millmead
Guildford
Surrey GU2 5BE
(0483) 504030

AUSTRALIA

**Auctioneers & Valuers Assoc. of
Australia (Inc)**
Suite 6, 3rd Flr
233 Macquarie Street
Sydney NSW 2000
(02) 235 2723

Christie's
298 New South Head Road
Double Bay NSW 2028
(02) 326 1422

Sotheby's Australia Pty. Ltd.
Head Office
13 Gurner Street
Paddington NSW 2021
(02) 332 3500

Christie's
103 Caroline Street
South Yarra VIC 3141
(03) 266 3715

Sotheby's Melbourne
606 High Street
East Prahran VIC 3181
(03) 529 7999

Christie's
346 Carrington Street
Adelaide SA 5000
(08) 232 2860

Sotheby's Agents

Richard Austin OBE
Rim House
Buderim QLD 4556
(071) 45 2171

Vanessa Wood
12 Altona Street
West Perth WA 6005
(09) 321 2354

Lawson's
212 Cumberland Street
Sydney NSW
(02) 241 3411

Art Met Gallery
Art Dealers
124 Jersey Road
Woollahra NSW 2025
(02) 32 9977

William Ellenden
Auctioneer
75 Mount Street
Coogee NSW 2034
(02) 665 5757

Edward Rushton Pty. Ltd.
184 Day Street
Darling Harbour NSW 2000
(02) 261 5533

CANADA

Pinney's Auctions Limited
5627 Ferrier
Montreal, Quebec H4P 2M4
(514) 731-4312

D. and J. Ritchie
429 Richmond Street East
Toronto, Ontario M5A 1R1
(416) 364-1864

Sotheby's
9 Hazelton Avenue
Toronto, Ontario M5R 2E1
(416) 926-1774

FRANCE

Hôtel Drouot
9 rue Drouot
Paris, France 75009
(331) 42-46-17-11
Most Paris auctions are held at this
location. The *Gazette de l'Hôtel
Drouot*, published weekly and sold at
newsstands, lists sale dates.

CONSERVATION AND RESTORATION

The care and preservation of fine antiques and art is an important part of collecting. Do consult an expert about the conservation of something you treasure.

The following organizations will provide a list of members for a fee:

American Institute for Conservation of Historic and Artistic Works
3545 Williamsburg Lane N.W.
Washington, DC 20008
(202) 364-1036

Conservation Unit
Museums and Galleries Commission
7 St. James's Square
London SW1Y 4JU

Conservation Bureau
Conservators and Restorers
Rosebery House, Haymarket Terrace
Edinburgh
(031) 337-9595

The British Antique Furniture Restorers' Association
37 Upper Addison Gardens
Holland Park
London W14 8AJ
(01) 603-5643

GREAT BRITAIN

Antique Leathers
4 Park End
South Hill Park
London NW3
(01) 435-8582   (leather)

The Castle Howard Textile Conservation Centre
York
(065) 384333   (textiles)

Carvers and Gilders
9 Charterhouse Works
Eltringham Street
London SW18
(01) 870-7047
  By appointment.

Francis Downing
The Studio
19 Lancaster Park Road
Harrogate, North Yorkshire
(0423) 886962   (paintings)

A. Dunn & Son, Marquetry
The White House
8 Wharf Road
Chelmsford
Essex
(0245) 354452   (wood)

Englefields, Pewterers
Reflection House
Cheshire Street
London E2
(01) 739-3616   (metals)

Jane McAusland
Nether Hall Barn
Old Newton
Stowmarket, Suffolk 1P14 4PP
(0449) 673571   (works on paper)

The Royal School of Needlework
25 Princes Gate
London SW7
(01) 589-0077   (textiles)

Spink's Furniture Restoration
5, 6, & 7 King Street
London SW1
(01) 930-7888   (wood)

St. Michael's Abbey Press
Farnborough, Hants
(0252) 547573   (books)

Eleanor Way
Wood Yard, Off Corve Street
Ludlow, Shropshire
(0584) 4654   (ceramics)

R. Wilkinson & Son
45 Wastdale Road
London SE23
(01) 699-4420   (glass)

Alan Winstanley, Bookbinding
213 Devizes Road
Salisbury, Wiltshire SP2 9LT
(0722) 334998   (books)

Barry Witmond
5A Mill Street
London W1
(01) 409-2335   (silver)

AUSTRALIA

Museums Association of Australia
Powerhouse Museum
500 Harris Street
Ultimo NSW
(02) 217 0133

Collectors can contact this organization to have their pieces restored or for restoration materials.

Australian Institute of Conservation of Cultural Material
P.O. Box 1638
Canberra ACT
(062) 414 044

This list of AICCM members is offered as a guide to restoration services and should not be seen as a recommendation by the Institute.

NSW

Ms Catherine Akeroyd
18 Eric Street
Lilyfield NSW 2040   (paper)

Mr Sellmas Andrewartha
1/47 Imperial Avenue
Bondi, NSW 2026   (works on paper, nontraditional paintings)

Mrs Gabriele J. Beatty
2/233A Johnstone Street
Annandale NSW 2038
(paper, paintings)

Mr David Beavis
Ravenswood Stained Glass
18 Main Street
Grenfell NSW 2810
(ecclesiastical stained glass)

Mr Ted Chapman
P.O. Box 25
Mulgoa NSW 2750   (books)

Mr Coenraad V. Hartman
Hartman Art Conservation
20 Barcod Street
Roseville NSW 2069
(stone, ceramics, glass)

Mr Richard S. McDonald
P.O. Box 13
Annandale NSW 2038
(paintings, textiles, books/paper)

Ms Heather McPherson
193 Rochford Street
Erskineville NSW 2043
(craft bookbinder)

Ms Angela Meeson
91 Paddington Street
Paddington NSW 2021
(paintings, sculpture, books/paper)

Mr John M. Opit
Limpinwood Fine Art Studio
P.O. Box 0
Tyalgum NSW 2484
(paintings, books/paper)

Ms Marion D. Ravenscroft
94 Barrenjoey Road
Palm Beach NSW 2108
(aboriginal carved trees and sites)

Ms Tessa M. Roberts
3/94 Kurraba Road
Neutral Bay NSW 2089
(tapestries and costume)

Ms Kay P. Soderlund
1/47 Glebe Point Road
Glebe NSW 2037   (paper)

Mr Paul E. Spratt
10 Stelling Avenue
Kanwal NSW 2259   (paintings)

Mr Graham Arthur David Whale
13 Young Street
Annandale NSW 2038   (ceramics)

Mr Douglas Zihrul
91 Eddy Road
Chatswood NSW 2067
(paintings, books/paper)

SA

Mr Keith Fernandez
State Conservation Centre
70 Kintore Avenue
Adelaide SA 5000
(paper, objects, paintings, textiles)

Mr Gwyn Kemp
40 Cooinda Avenue
Redwood Park SA 5097   (furniture, objects, horological objects)

Mr Geoffrey Lewis
P.O. Box 25
Langhorne Creek SA 5255
(ceramics)

VIC

Mr John C. Alexander
J. C. Alexander and Associates
12 Mary Street
West St Kilda VIC 3182
(paintings, ethno-archaeological objects)

Mrs Beatrice E. Burgemeestre
Fine Art Restoration
6 High Street
Kew VIC 3101
(paintings, works on paper)

Mr Maxwell A. Hall
17 Arundel Crescent
Surrey Hills VIC 3127
(paintings, paper)

Mr John R. Perry
Rear, 1 Molesworth Street
Hawthorn East VIC 3123
(paintings)

Mr Charles Philipp
68 Armadale Street
Armadale VIC 3143   (ceramics)

Ms Elizabeth G. Pilven
4 Chamouni Street
Alphington VIC 3078   (textiles)

Mr Martin Tomlinson
12 Mary Street
St Kilda West VIC 3182
(oriental textiles, ceramics, metals)

Mr Edmund Valentin
66 Kinkora Road
Hawthorn VIC 3122
(paintings, paper)

Mr George Vlahogiannis
32 Bastings Street
Northcote VIC 3070
(furniture, wooden artifacts)

Ms Louise Young
63 Fairbairn Road
Toorak VIC 3142   (paper)

WA

Mrs R. J. Car
288 Mouatt Street
Fremantle WA 6160   (textiles, objects, ethnographic objects)

Mrs Patricia E. Moncrieff
P.O. Box 615
Fremantle WA 6160   (textiles)

Mrs Margaret A. Myers
77 Falls Road
Lesmurdie WA 6076   (objects)

QLD

Mr Richard Allom
Allom, Lovell, Marquis-Kyle P/L
P.O. Box 431
Fortitude Valley QLD 4006
(architectural materials)

Ms Vicki Locke
P.O. Box 75
Mapleton QLD 4560
(paintings, textiles, paper/books)

Ms Nan Paterson
P.O. Box 422
Maleny QLD 4552   (paintings)

Mr William K. Richardson
110 Andrew Street
Wynnum QLD 4178
(paintings, paper)

TAS

Mr Michael R. Chambers
P.O. Box 38
Westbury TAS 7303   (wooden objects, architectural materials)

ACT

Ms Carol Cains
31 Herbert Crescent
Ainslie ACT 2602   (textiles)

Mrs Susan M. Ride Gaardboe
5 Francis Street
Yarralumla ACT 2600
(textiles, ethnographic objects)

Ms Robin M. Tait
P.O. Box 43
Watson ACT 2602   (books)

MAGAZINES AND PERIODICALS

An important part of collecting
is keeping up with what is happening in the international art and
decorative arts world. A good
way to do this is to read one or
more of the magazines and peri-
odicals devoted to the arts.

The Antique Collector
Freepost 25
London W1
(01) 439-7144

**The Antique Dealer and
Collectors' Guide**
Room 2427, King's Reach Tower
Stamford Street
London SE1
(01) 261-6844

Apollo
P.O. Box 47
North Hollywood, CA 91603
(818) 763-7673

Art & Antiques
89 Fifth Avenue
New York, NY 10003
(212) 206-7050

Art & Auction
250 West 57th Street
New York, NY 10019
(212) 582-5633

Australian Antique Collector
162 Goulburn Street
Darlinghurst NSW 2010
(02) 266 9711

Australian Antique Trader
250 Military Road
Neutral Bay NSW 2089
(02) 905 1588

**The Australian Collector's
Quarterly**
54 Park Street
Sydney NSW 2000
(02) 282 8300

Belle
54 Park Street, 5th Floor
Sydney NSW 2000
(02) 282 8000

Better Homes and Gardens
14 Herbert Street
Artamon NSW 2064
(02) 437 4999

The Burlington Magazine
6 Bloomsbury Square
London WC1
(01) 430-0481

Casa Vogue
27 Piazza Castello
Milan, Italy 20121
(02) 85-611

Connaissance des Arts
25 rue de Ponthieu
Paris, France 75008
(01) 43-59-62-00

Connoisseur
The Hearst Corporation
959 Eighth Avenue
New York, NY 10019
(212) 957-4119

Country Life
Oakfield House
35 Perrymount Road
Haywards Heath
West Sussex
(0444) 459188

Good Housekeeping
54 Park Street, 2nd Floor
Sydney NSW 2000
(02) 282 8000

Home Beautiful (Australia)
32 Walsh Street
West Melbourne VIC 3003
(03) 320 7020

Homes and Living (Australia)
1 Leonard Street
Victoria Park WA 6100
(09) 362 6711

House and Garden (Australia)
54 Park Street
Sydney NSW 2000
(02) 282 8000

House & Garden (British)
Oakfield House
35 Perrymount Road
Haywards Heath
West Sussex
(0444) 440421

House Beautiful
1700 Broadway
New York, NY 10019
(212) 903-5100

Living with Antiques
250 Military Road
Neutral Bay NSW 2089
(02) 905 1588

The Magazine Antiques
Old Mill Road, P.O. Box 1975
Marion, OH 43305
(800) 247-2160

Maison & Jardin
10 Boulevard du Montparnasse
Paris, France 75015
(1) 45-67-35-05

Vogue Décoration
10 Boulevard du Montparnasse
Paris, France 75015
(1) 45-67-35-05

Vogue Living
170 Pacific Highway
Greenwich NSW 2065
(02) 964 3888

The World of Interiors
234 Kings Road
London SW3
(01) 351-5177

SOCIETIES AND ORGANIZATIONS

There are many wonderful organizations that you can join to learn about the decorative arts. As a member, you will not only be meeting people with the same interests as you, but you will also be able to participate in the programs and attend the lectures the society offers.

UNITED STATES

National Trust for Historic Preservation (U.S.)
Member Services
1785 Massachusetts Avenue N.W.
Washington, DC 20036
(202) 673-4129

GREAT BRITAIN

Antique Collectors Club
5 Church Street
Woodbridge
Suffolk 1P12 1DS
(0394) 385501

Architectural Heritage Society Scotland
43B Manor Place
Edinburgh EH3 7EB
(031) 225-9724

Georgian Group
37 Spital Square
London E1 6DY
(01) 377-1722

The National Trust
36 Queen Anne's Gate
London SW1H 9AF
(01) 222-9251

Regency Society of Brighton and Hove
38 Prince Regent's Close
Brighton BN2 5JP
(0273) 606881

Thirties Society
3 Park Square West
London NW1 4LJ
(01) 486-3805

Victorian Society
1 Priory Gardens
London W4 1TT
(01) 994-1019

AUSTRALIA

Antique Dealers Guild of Australia
(07) 369 4433

Historic Houses Trust of NSW
(02) 692 8366

Museums Association of Australia
(02) 217 0133

National Trust
(02) 258 0128

NSW Antique Dealers Association
(02) 660 3019

Victorian Antique Dealers Association
(03) 654 5903

South Australian Antique Dealers Association
(08) 231 0101

Queensland Antique Dealers Association
(07) 391 6919

Tasmanian Antique Dealers Association
(003) 911 571

BOOKSELLERS

The firms and individual booksellers listed carry a varied selection of old and new books on the decorative and fine arts. Many have mail-order catalogs.

UNITED STATES

Ars Libri
560 Harrison Avenue
Boston, MA 02118
(617) 357-5212

Timothy Mawson Books
Main Street
New Preston, CT 06777
(203) 868-0732

Timothy Trace Booksellers
144 Red Mill Road
Peekskill, NY 10566
(914) 528-4074

Ursus Books and Prints
981 Madison Avenue
New York, NY 10021
(212) 772-8787

GREAT BRITAIN

Thomas Heneage & Company
42 Duke Street
London SW1
(01) 720-1503

John Ives
5 Normanhurst Drive
Twickenham
Middlesex
(01) 892-6265

Don Kelly Books
Stand M13, Antiquarius
135 Kings Road
London SW3
(01) 352-4690

Maggs Brothers
50 Berkeley Square
London W1
(01) 493-7160

Potterton Books
The Old Rectory
Sessay
North Yorkshire
(0845) 401218

AUSTRALIA

All State Art Galleries have bookshops with a wide range of books on the fine and decorative arts. National Trust bookshops in each state generally carry a good selection on the decorative arts, particularly Australiana.

Sydney

All Arts Bookshop
160 Oxford Street
Woollahra NSW 2025
(02) 328 6774

Angus & Robertson Bookshop
Imperial Arcade
168 Pitt Street
Sydney NSW 2000
(02) 235 1188

Ariel Booksellers
42 Oxford Street
Paddington NSW 2021
(02) 332 4581

Bibliophile Old Books and Prints
24 Glenmore Road
Paddington NSW 2021
(02) 331 1411

The Building Bookshop
525 Elizabeth Street
Surry Hills NSW 2010
(02) 699 5435

Hordern House
77 Victoria Street
Potts Point NSW 2011
(02) 356 4411

Louella Kerr Books
26 Glenmore Road
Paddington NSW 2021
(02) 33 4664

Nicholas Pounder Bookseller
298 Victoria Road
Kings Cross NSW 2011
(02) 331 5480

Melbourne

Art Salon
5 Crossley Street
Melbourne VIC 3000
(03) 662 2918

The Arts Bookshop Pty. Ltd.
1067 High Street
Armadale VIC 3143
(03) 20 2645

Gallery Art Naive
457 Malvern Road
South Yarra VIC 3141
(03) 240 8551

Hill of Content Bookshop
86 Bourke Street
Melbourne VIC 3000
(03) 654 3144

National Gallery Bookshop
Victoria Arts Centre
St. Kilda Road
Melbourne VIC 3000
(03) 618 0222

Peter Arnold
463 High Street
Prahan VIC 3181
(03) 529-2933

Readings
153 Toorak Road
South Yarra VIC 3141
(03) 266 8586

Webber's Bookshop
15 McKillop Street
Melbourne VIC 3000
(03) 670 2418

Whole Earth Bookshop
83 Bourke Street
Melbourne VIC 3000
(03) 650 9292

SUGGESTED READING

Learning about antiques is one of the pleasures of collecting. There are many excellent books, both old and new, that cover every imaginable topic. Here are those that I have mentioned within the chapters of this book.

Ames, Frank. *The Kashmir Shawl.* Woodbridge, England: The Antique Collectors Club, 1986.

Benjamin, Susan. *English Enamel Boxes from the Eighteenth to the Twentieth Centuries.* London: Orbis Publishing Ltd., 1978.

Blair, Matthew. *The Paisley Shawl.* Paisley, England: Alexander Gardner, 1904.

Bradbury, Frederick, compiler. *Bradbury's Book of Hallmarks.* Sheffield, England: J. W. Northend, Ltd., 1968.

Carter, Mary E. *Millionaire Households.* New York: D. Appleton and Co., 1903.

Chaffers, William. *Marks and Monograms on European and Oriental Pottery and Porcelain.* Los Angeles: Borden, 1946.

Cornforth, John. *The Inspiration of the Past.* New York: Viking Press, 1985.

Cotterell, Howard Herschel. *Old Pewter: Its Makers and Marks.* Rutland, Vermont: Charles E. Tuttle Co., 1963.

Cripps, Wilfred Joseph. *Old English Plate.* London: John Murray, 1881.

Cushion, J. P., and W. B. Honey. *Handbook of Pottery and Porcelain Marks.* London: Faber & Faber, 1980.

Earnshaw, Pat. *The Identification of Lace.* England: Shire Publications, 1980.

Eastlake, Charles Locke. *Hints on Household Taste.* Boston: James R. Osgood & Co., 1872.

Ensko, Stephen G. C. *American Silversmiths and Their Marks.* New York: Robert Ensko, Inc., 1937.

Godden, Geoffrey A. *Encyclopedia of British Pottery and Porcelain Marks.* New York: Crown, 1976. Reprint. New York: Salem House Ltd./Seven Hills Books, 1984.

Jackson, Charles J. *English Goldsmiths and Their Marks.* 1923. Reprint. New York: Dover Publications, 1964.

———. *The Illustrated History of English Plate.* 1911. Reprint. New York: Dover Publications, 1969.

Kovel, Ralph M. and Terry H. *Dictionary of Marks—Pottery and Porcelain.* New York: Crown Publishers, Inc., 1953.

Laughlin, Ledlie Irwin. *Pewter in America.* Boston: Houghton, Mifflin, 1940.

Lee, Ruth Webb. *Early American Pressed Glass.* Framingham, Massachusetts: Lee Publications, 1931.

Little, Nina Fletcher. *Neat and Tidy.* New York: E. P. Dutton, 1980.

Macquoid, Percy, and Ralph Edwards. *The Dictionary of English Furniture.* 3 vols., 1924–1927. Revised by Ralph Edwards. London: Country Life Ltd., 1983.

Mayor, A. Hyatt. *Prints and People.* New York: The Metropolitan Museum of Art, 1971.

Nutting, Wallace. *Furniture Treasury.* 3 vols. New York: Macmillan & Co., 1933, 1988.

Palliser, Mrs. Bury. *The History of Lace.* England: Sampson Low, 1910.

Poe, Edgar Allan. "The Philosophy of Furniture." 1840. Reprint, excerpts, *House and Garden* (April 1924), 90, 136.

Praz, Mario. *An Illustrated History of Interior Decoration.* New York: Thames & Hudson, 1982.

Reighe, Emily. *An Illustrated Guide to Lace.* Woodbridge, England: The Antique Collectors Club, 1986.

Ring, Betty. *American Needlework Treasures.* New York: E. P. Dutton, 1987.

Sack, Albert. *Fine Points of Furniture: Early American.* New York: Crown Publishers, 1950.

Sack, Harold, and Max Wilk. *American Treasure Hunt.* New York: Ballantine Books, 1986.

Seligman, Germain. *Merchants of Art, 1880–1960: Eighty Years of Professional Collecting.* New York: Appleton-Century-Crofts, 1961.

Sloane, Eric. *A Reverence for Wood.* 1965. Reprint. New York: Ballantine Books, 1973.

Sprigg, June. *By Shaker Hands.* New York: Alfred A. Knopf, Inc., 1975.

Swan, Susan Burrows. *Plain and Fancy.* New York: Holt, Rinehart and Winston, 1977.

Thornton, Peter. *Authentic Decor: The Domestic Interior.* New York: Viking Press, 1984.

Wharton, Edith, and Ogden Cogman. *The Decoration of Houses.* 1897/1914. Reprint. New York: Arno Press, 1975.

Zerwick, Chloe. *A Short History of Glass.* Corning, New York: The Corning Museum, 1980.

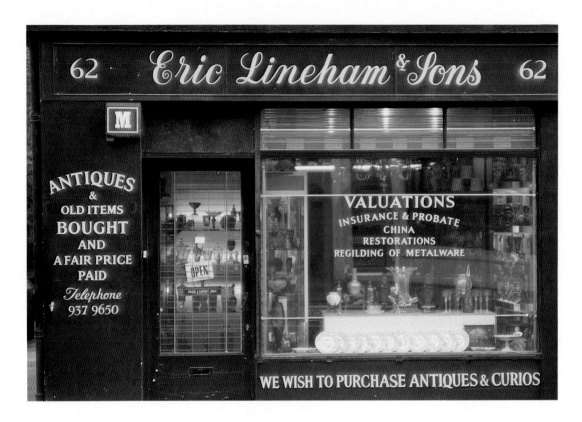

INDEX